THE **END** OF
COMPETITION

The Impact of the Network Economy

THE END OF COMPETITION

The Impact of the Network Economy

COR MOLENAAR

Erasmus University Rotterdam, The Netherlands

 World Scientific

EW JERSEY • LONDON • SINGAPORE • BEIJING • SHANGHAI • HONG KONG • TAIPEI • CHENNAI • TOKYO

Published by

World Scientific Publishing Co. Pte. Ltd.

5 Toh Tuck Link, Singapore 596224

USA office: 27 Warren Street, Suite 401-402, Hackensack, NJ 07601

UK office: 57 Shelton Street, Covent Garden, London WC2H 9HE

Library of Congress Cataloging-in-Publication Data
Names: Molenaar, Cor, author.
Title: The end of competition : the impact of the network economy /
    Cor Molenaar, Erasmus University Rotterdam, The Netherlands.
Description: Singapore ; Hackensack, NJ : World Scientific Publishing Co. Pte. Ltd., [2020] |
    Includes bibliographical references and index.
Identifiers: LCCN 2019053557 | ISBN 9789811212314 (hardcover) |
    ISBN 9789811212321 (ebook)
Subjects: LCSH: Competition. | Business networks. | Business--Technological innovations.
Classification: LCC HB238 .M65 2020 | DDC 658.4/06--dc23
LC record available at https://lccn.loc.gov/2019053557

British Library Cataloguing-in-Publication Data
A catalogue record for this book is available from the British Library.

For any available supplementary material, please visit
https://www.worldscientific.com/worldscibooks/10.1142/11608#t=suppl

Desk Editors: Balasubramanian/Karimah Samsudin

Typeset by Stallion Press
Email: enquiries@stallionpress.com

Printed in Singapore by Mainland Press Pte Ltd.

Despite all the technology it always comes down to customers, people of flesh and blood with their own emotions.

Co Konijn (2000)

Preface

The frictions that we experience when doing business, and in fact also in society, result from the impact of technology. There is a transition period from 'doing digital' to 'being digital'. This affects every aspect of our lives, both private and professional. Merely observing the changes, reading about conflicts of the old model in relation to the new model, is confusing. The current developments and frictions require more in-depth examination. Insights into these developments will be necessary in order to achieve success. Many more partnerships will develop; organisations will come together and combine forces and borders will disappear. This will lead to the changes from order entry to new digital business ecosystems, or rather from 'doing digital' to 'being digital'.

How is it that these new concepts can suddenly grow so quickly (network effects)? And that the international growth is a question of months, or even shorter, where previously it required decades or longer? And how is it that new businesses can continue to exist despite massive losses? The transition from a transaction-based model to a value model requires modifications in the organisation, in the focus as well as in the strategy. We suddenly see old terms being used such as 'commodification', a term that was important for Karl Marx, which indicates that each transaction is a value component. So why then are prices determined on the basis of an exchange of products (transaction-oriented) and not on the basis of budgets (value-oriented)? This change alone requires a new vision, whereby old criteria and (marketing) instruments have to be modified on the basis of a value exchange.

This also explains the discussions on returning articles from online sales in this transition period. In the traditional model, the buyer was the weaker party and had to be protected with legislation and guarantees. However, with the new resources, technology forms the basis. Purchases made through digital media may be returned within two weeks in Europe. But why two weeks? Why can items that have clearly been used be returned, and why do potential buyers order so many articles that they later send back? Customers are abusing the new possibilities and the old legislation. This is a change from '*caveat emptor*' to '*caveat venditor*'. A shift of dependency, from the customer to the supplier. I have actually not come across these terms in the marketing literature. Blockchain can lead to modifications in this.

A study into buying motives and buying behaviour has led to new insights that form the basis of the current changes. The necessity to buy has disappeared and has been replaced by a choice in what is bought and where. In the old, supply-based model it is all to do with comparative cost advantages. The price as a weapon against the competition. This involved protecting markets against new entrants, international suppliers and substitute products. Defence as the basis for success. These days this protective approach is no longer workable; defence leads to shrinkage and eventual disappearance. Also relevant these days are buying motives and motivating customers to buy. It comes down to developing a vision of value exchange instead of price. But what does a customer actually buy? The product, the service, the imaginary value, the experience or the acceptance within an intended group? Businesses have to delve deeper into these, often individual, buying motives. New analysis systems based on artificial intelligence are necessary, and lead to the formulation of algorithms. The future competition will no longer be about comparative competitive advantages but will involve customer loyalty and algorithms. These are new technological applications that will form the basis of doing business. And this change process has only just begun.

Many companies are still busy optimising or digitalising the current processes (doing digital), although this is based on an outdated, traditional model, with a supply chain, the sale of services and a customer journey. New concepts, however, are rapidly conquering markets, such as Airbnb, Uber, dating sites, booking.com, Deliveroo and many more. These involve new revenue models, strong market positions and are based on collaboration. Existing organisations can no longer compete with these. Complaints and bans are only temporary solutions. Often the management is so restricted by old regulations, outdated KPIs and a redundant pursuit of profits that it is difficult, if not impossible, to adapt. So the question is, what sort of future do these businesses have? Should they join existing platforms, develop one's own platform or become a niche player?

Customers do not let themselves be pushed anymore, and loyalty systems that reward transactions no longer lead to the desired impulses. A 'net promoter score' is too subjective to base any policy on it; data analyses, on the other hand, are objective. But a customer also has to want to feel loyal to a product, brand or supplier. An affinity. A positive feeling. After all, isn't there a positive feeling about the sponsor of your sports club? Creating an affinity requires direct and personalised communication. And for this you need algorithms. Platforms will attract and create a bond with visitors, but products and services have to motivate them.

The constant denial of these developments, the continual trivialising of platforms, because they would lead to unfair competition (!) or acquire a dominant market position (such as with Alibaba.com or Amazon.com) is surely a sign of impotence? Not wanting to change and refusing to respond to the wishes of consumers?

We are shifting from a supply-driven economy to a demand-driven economy, you could say a Fourth Industrial Revolution. Taking part is no longer a choice; it is a necessity. But how, when and with what technology or partners? With which partners and in what concept (platform)? In this book I explore the indicators of change, the motives for change and the changes that are yet to come. Concrete plans provide clarity regarding the steps that can be taken, and they indicate who is already going down that road. It took a thorough theoretical analysis to determine the current developments and to predict any future ones. In my book, *The End of Shops* (2011), based on buying behaviour I predicted that many shops would disappear due to their decreasing relevance with the new buying behaviour. In 2017, I analysed the disruptive nature of platforms. These platforms, like Uber and Airbnb actually only emerged after 2015 based on new automation possibilities such as multiservice programming, APIs and new analysis techniques. My conclusion was and remains, **it is bend or break**. In the last two years, I have been involved in various change strategies in the course of which platforms and algorithms based on analyses were developed. This has lead not only to new insights and knowledge but also to an increasing realisation that much more still needs to be done.

The developments in the Western world are influenced by the freedom of choice people enjoy, cultural aspects and the adoption of new technologies. In Asia we see not only some similar developments but also developments that are different. In particular due to the Internet penetration later taking on larger forms, it was possible to make modifications to the concept. In many Asian countries such as China, South Korea and Vietnam, their governments take on a much more intensive role than in the Western world. We see other developments as a result, and also typically European issues such as privacy are dealt with differently in Asian countries. This leads to a stimulus in innovative applications, such as social media, virtual reality and commercial applications like face recognition and algorithms. I devote a separate chapter in this book to examine the social media in Asia and its consequences.

With a group of eMarketing students from the Rotterdam School of Management at Erasmus University in the Netherlands, I have carried out research in the Netherlands and Europe as well as in Asia and, in particular, in America. The current developments are universal. In this book, I make various references to these studies and to study trips to, for example, America, China and South Korea. I would like to draw particular attention to a number of studies and researchers: Tim Scholtes and Jan Biezepol: *The Future of Competition*; Henrique Campos; Wael Romdhane and Pierre Vigor: *Integration Online and Offline in a Physical World*; Erik Casemier and Eline van Groningen: *What is the Impact of the Matching Function on Multisided Platforms on the Customer Experience*; Zuzana Kupcova, Paul Chaintreuil and Guilia Montorsi: *How do Consumers Behavior and Loyalty Change in a Network Economy*; Richelle Lum Shun Yi, Kristel Tan Sheng Hui and Pim Fijt: *The Future of Retailing for both Traditional and Platform Retailers*; Wendy-Kristy Hoogerbrugge (OU): *Over Inbound Marketing and Innovation* and Chrystalla Panteli, Songri Lee and Subin Jeon: *Target Marketing by the US, South Korea and China*. The chapter about Asia was written in close cooperation with Songri Lee and Subin Jeon. I also like to mention Sofie Geeroms (asbl BeCommerce vzw). During our study trip in China we discussed thoroughly the impact of all new developments. It really sharpened my insight and vision.

In addition, I have had many discussions with Ruben Schmetz on the automation aspects, and have met with potential suppliers of platform technology with API links (there are not that many). With Meindert van Duyvenbode from Datacon, I have developed various concepts and talked about certain limitations of systems. During our study trip to China, I had the opportunity to discuss the developments from a practical point of view with Dick Slootweg from Bidfood. I also greatly appreciated his valuable constructive criticisms on the manuscript. Regarding the modifications for the section about Asia, eMarketing exchange students Songri Lee and Subin Jeon provided me with much support in the analyses as well as many opportunities for discussions.

And finally, I would like to thank my wife Patricia, the basis for all these studies. It is often a giant leap from planet Cor to earth. But just the occasional comment was usually enough.

I have greatly enjoyed gathering and analysing the data as well as putting it into a practical context. During this process I have become convinced that we are at the beginning of a new age: **the age of 'being digital'**, with other rules, other suppliers and a different buying behaviour. Closing your eyes to this is to deny yourself a future.

C.N.A. Molenaar
Oosterbeek
May 2019
Email: cor@cormolenaar.nl
Websites: www.exquo.nl; www.platformsupport.nl

About the Author

Cor Molenaar is Professor at RSM/Erasmus University in Rotterdam for the chair eMarketing. He is also founder and director of the consultancy-bureau eXQuo consultancy and Platformsupport.nl in The Netherlands. He is an authority on the field of digitalisation in Marketing and the impact of platforms on business structures and competitive strategies.

He is an advisor to various big and medium size companies in Europe and a frequently asked speaker on conferences and board room sessions.

Contents

Preface   vii

About the Author   xiii

Chapter 1   Introduction   1

Chapter 2   The Development of the Network Economy:
             Opportunities and Threats   7

Chapter 3   The New Market Conditions   33

Chapter 4   From Supply Chain to Network   51

Chapter 5   Networks Become the Competition   81

Chapter 6   Technology as a Basis for New Competitive
             Relationships   109

Chapter 7   It is about Customers, Not Products: A Change
             of Vision   131

Chapter 8   New Marketing and Competition Principles
             through the Adoption of Technology   145

Chapter 9   Opportunities for Asia Based on Characteristics
             and Culture   161

Chapter 10   Towards the Future: Join In or Disappear?   201

Appendix 1   *Bidfood: Development and Platform Strategy
             Rollout*   219

Appendix 2   *Dating Sites: An Example of a Multisided Platform* 227

Appendix 3   *Differences between Various Forms of Collaboration* 231

Chapter 1

Introduction

There is a clear change in the success formulas of businesses. The strength of the largest industrial companies, such as Philips, Unilever or General Electric, used to be based on economies of scale on the supply side of the economy. These companies achieved their market power through managing resources, internally optimising processes and expanding their customer base using a competitive pricing strategy. Vertical integration and mergers and acquisitions ensured there was greater control across the entire value chain. Since the Industrial Revolution this has been the strategy for generating comparative competitive advantages. At the end of the last century, successful businesses still operated using a classical linear value chain, whereby a series of consecutive value activities was carried out and all production processes were controlled primarily from the company itself. For many years, the markets, both physical and local, were aimed at *business-to-consumer* (B2C) sales.

Since the beginning of the 21st century, the basic strategic principles have changed. The fastest growing companies of this century, Google, Facebook, Apple, Uber, Alibaba and Airbnb, operate in a different way.

These platform companies bring together supply and demand with efficient exchanges of value. But haven't these types of companies always existed? After all, markets and shopping centres bring consumers

1

in contact with traders, newspapers connect subscribers and advertisers, travel agents help tourists find suitable holidays and dating sites match singles looking for a partner. What has actually changed in the last few years is that information technology has greatly reduced the need for physical assets and has enabled these business models to develop to a global scale. The dating app Tinder has a *worldwide* online database of singles in contrast to local dating agencies. Uber and Didi in China don't actually own any cars by themselves but connect consumers looking for a lift with drivers. Airbnb connects hosts and guests without possessing any rooms itself, thereby competing with, for example, Marriott hotel, which has extremely high overheads due to its ownership of hotels and employment of staff. Walmart has one of the best stock control and logistics operations, but Alibaba has significantly increased its value without having any inventory at all. As external producers are able to add value to the platform (supply), a comparable value proposition can be realised for the consumer (demand), without the platform company having any control over the production process. This is what makes platform companies so disruptive.

How can we explain the rapid domination of these companies? In order to understand how the emergence of platforms has transformed competition strategies, it's important to illustrate the differences between classic businesses and platform businesses.

The driving force behind our network economy is now being created by generating economies of scale on the demand side of the economy, known as network effects. These network effects arise when users create value for other users. The larger the network, the richer the data coming from the online interaction between supply and demand, and the better the matching functionality of the platform, the more valuable the underlying platform is for users on both sides of the market. And this in turn will attract more users. The literature describes this phenomenon as the network effect. It enables platform companies to grow exponentially instead of linearly, the way traditional companies do. When a linear organisation gains a new customer, this results in just one additional business relationship, one extra transaction. In a platform organisation, on the other hand, a new consumer is able to enter into a business relationship with every single producer on that platform.

The most important competitive advantage of a platform is the network of producers and consumers that creates value for one another and can exchange this value by means of the platform (Choudary, 2015).

The emergence of business ecosystems and platforms represents a very recent development that has a considerable effect on traditional industries and product and service markets. Platform businesses differ significantly in terms of market potential, structure and management approaches compared with product and service businesses. The differences conflict with the traditional management assumptions, in particular regarding property and control. The growth in acceptance of platform business models is not only a challenge for established businesses but also raises questions regarding the instruments and techniques that are currently used for strategic decision-making and the underlying traditional value chain.

The competition between businesses will change because customer behaviour is changing and because the technology is available.

Those who believe in the future of the network economy and platforms and think they can boost their competitive strength by aligning themselves to these will find it easier to adapt and can help to bring about the shift in the entire sector. But those who do not believe in a future of networks or platforms and believe they will become victims of this new competition will fight against the change and lose their competitive edge. Depending on what the majority think and how customers will respond, companies that resist may very well disappear in a world in which networks and platforms assume power. Companies that are too frightened or rigid to change or aren't really sure what to do will wait too long to carry out the necessary changes and suffer the consequences. They can take the initiative themselves and respond to the changes or become part of a platform. Joining a dominant disruptor is then an option for companies, if they aren't able to do it independently or feel they are not able to fight against the new, large suppliers. It is then truly a question of bend or break.

The future remains open for the time being. The answers to the changes depend on our choices. Our future will be determined by the manner in which we deploy and use technology. These choices will be made in a world that is inherently in flux and ever-changing and will be formed, at least to a certain extent, on the basis of the unpredictable technological changes and how we respond to them. In short, the changes in the market depend on how the customers adopt the new developments and how new market structures are accepted.

Networks, such as platforms, increase the competition for traditional suppliers and make it more transparent. This has consequences for both customers and suppliers. Customers will benefit from not only more suppliers and products from which they can choose but also from the transparency. The suppliers have a higher turnover because they are able to sell more due to a stronger marketing strategy and new propositions such as home deliveries. Customers have more information about their order and a better overview of what is on offer as well as the prices. Factors such as saving time, freedom of choice and speed of delivery are very important when it comes to attracting customers, and so platforms and networks try to keep the information up-to-date. They want to aim their communication specifically at the individuals they target using all sorts of algorithms in order to retain the loyalty of and provide service to businesses and customers. Through a platform, suppliers are able to benefit from the appeal of the network, the customer loyalty and the joint approach to the market. This not only saves costs but also immediately increases the competitive strength (the network effect). Collaboration is the basis for the future.

Shift 1: Competitive Strengths are Used in the Platform Business Model

Platform businesses facilitate the interactions between producers and consumers, whereby the greatest part of the value is created through this network of external users of the platform. The focus in terms of strategy thereby shifts from internal optimisation to a maximisation of external interaction.

Shift 2: From Ownership to a Coordination of Resources

The resource-based view focuses the attention of the management on the company's internal resources in order to identify those assets, capacities and competences that have the potential to gain competitive advantages. These are resources that the company owns and/or controls. In linear companies, these resources would be tangible assets such as factories, equipment and raw materials and intangible resources such as brands and intellectual property. In contrast to traditional businesses, platform companies do not produce products and/or provide services themselves; production processes are not organised by the organisation, and as a result, there is no control of the creation of value within the production process. This value is brought in by external producers and coordinated by the platform company. The network of external producers and consumers is the most important capital of the platform company.

Shift 3: From a Focus on Customer Value to One on the Value of Ecosystems

Linear companies with traditional strategic models aim to maximise the *lifetime value* of individual customers of products and/or services. These customers are located at the end of the linear process — B2C. Platforms, on the contrary, want to maximise the total value of a growing network, whereby that network consists of users who supply a product or service on the one hand and users who consume that product or service on the other. The users can exchange roles or carry out various roles simultaneously. Eisenmann *et al.* (2006) suggest that because platforms have a different group of users on either side, the value creation shifts from left to right and from right to left. Users of Uber, for example, may take a taxi ride one day and be a taxi driver the next; travellers may stay the night at an Airbnb on one occasion but then host an Airbnb on another. This change in the value chain is an important feature of a two-sided market.

Amazon under Fire in Austria

Austrian retailers have lodged a complaint against Amazon with the federal competition authority. The retailers have highlighted the double role of the American webstore and the growing domination in the Austrian market. They want to eliminate 'disruptive trade conditions' and call for fair competition.

European Doubts about Amazon

The role of Amazon is under fire in other European markets as well. The European commission is investigating, for example, whether the webstore uses the data of retailers selling their products via the Amazon platform for its own personal gain (*Het Financieele Dagblad*, 10 December 2018, fd.nl/krant/2018/12/10).

Bibliography

Choudary, S. P. (2015). *Platform Scale*. Platform Thinking Labs.
Eisenmann, T. R., Parker, G., and Van Alstyne, M. W. (2006). Strategies for two sided markets. *Harvard Business Review*. Available at: SSRN: https://ssrn.com/abstract=2409276.

Chapter 2

The Development of the Network Economy: Opportunities and Threats

How Powerful are the New Platforms?

Facebook CEO, Mark Zuckerberg, had to defend himself in front of the American Congress. Facebook had not been keeping a close enough eye on the messages and advertisements on its platform. This enabled information and messages to be manipulated (*fake news*), possibly also during the American 2016 presidential election. Facebook's use of data left behind by 'friends', which were analysed in order to allow for targeted advertising, also faced criticism. The fact that no one pays for Facebook led to questions about its business model: '4.3 billion dollars profit while users don't pay?'

The older decision-makers and leaders showed considerable ignorance regarding the new platforms. Facebook has 3.5 billion users worldwide and is by far the largest social medium outside China. In China, WeChat is the largest with over 1 billion users, and the company is growing rapidly. This development is particularly spectacular because WeChat only started in 2011 while Facebook began in 2004. Thanks to all the contacts that a person accumulates, the unprecedented power of the market leader,

Facebook, is immense. It is not easy to leave this platform because then you would 'lose all your friends' who do decide to stay on the platform (*prisoner's dilemma*). Through this phenomenon, Facebook has all but acquired a monopoly whereby other social media can be no more than a niche player (such as Twitter, Instagram, part of Facebook, and LinkedIn, part of Microsoft).

Google also gets a great deal of criticism for its market position. As a search engine, it has almost a complete monopoly in Europe with a 95% market share. In the Netherlands, this is as much as 98.8% for the smartphone and 89.3% for the computer. This dominant position leads to irritation in the European Union and has resulted in a €2.4 billion fine. But is this dominant position of 'Google Search' not the fault of the European Union's passive attitude? Google is also the market leader in the United States, but with a much lower market share of 63.5%, alongside the 24% market share of Microsoft and the 11.4% market share of Oath (formerly Yahoo). In the last 20 years, Europe has not developed any alternative to the new platforms and is trying through fines to slow down this development without offering any alternatives. Competing with Google Search is actually impossible due to its name recognition, the sophisticated algorithms and the many embedded applications.

The fine in 2017 (€2.4 billion) was all to do with the strength of the Google search engine coupled with the lack of competition. Google Shopping was always at the top of the search results. This was seen as Google abusing its dominant position. In 2018, it received another fine; this time €4.34 billion for making it compulsory for manufacturers of smartphones to install the Google search engine on the phone's (Google) Android operating system. This made it impossible for other search engines to compete with Google Search. Apple has its own system (iOS) so this did not count. These are all signs of old regulations and an old vision on competition in a new world. Buyers and customers don't mind this 'monopoly'; they don't pay for it and actually often find it convenient. The competition, however, is excluded, as they aren't able to offer any additional value. Is this a taste of what competition will be like in the network economy? Or is it in fact a different sort of competition, the scope of which we are as yet not aware of? It is striking that there seems to be the illusion that customers don't have enough choice due to the new dominant positions, while customers don't experience it as such. After all, in the physical world the choice is limited and specific to location or country.

Uber and Airbnb also experience a great deal of opposition from the traditional suppliers and legislators. Uber is popular as a taxi business due to its good service, reliability and transparency, both in terms of price and route. Traditional taxi businesses, which work with licenses, feel threatened because customers prefer to use the Uber ride. Does it then not make sense that traditional taxi companies should also integrate these useful functionalities: an app, transparency, clear routes and automatic payments? The unwillingness to compete with the new entrants (Uber) is a typical response; ban the competition rather than adapt to change. However, considering the preference shown by customers, participating with the Uber concept is the only possibility for successful competition.

Airbnb is facing similar opposition. This hospitality platform where private individuals can offer lodgings to other individuals is now immensely popular due to its small scale, low costs and flexibility. Many tourists no longer want the luxury of a hotel but prefer a place to stay without all the bells and whistles. The popularity of Airbnb is leading to more tourists visiting popular cities such as New York, London, Amsterdam and Barcelona. But as the homes of private individuals are used for lodging, this also leads to resistance.

Limited legal restrictions can be appropriate at times; however, stringent regulations, or even bans, simply serve to resist the inevitable change. The resistance primarily comes from the strong lobby from hotels, which are seeing some of their profits disappear. But what we don't see is a change in the business strategy in response to the wishes of the customers. This is even leading to Airbnb (probably) being banned in New York because hotels regard this as unfair competition. These tourists bring in money and help to stimulate employment and the economy. This leads to an extra financial impulse among private individuals who rent out a room or apartment. It is a double-edged sword; it is not the large hotels that profit from the tourists but private individuals and small and medium-sized businesses. The traditional providers, such as hotels, can still offer customers what they have always provided when it comes to 'all the bells and whistles' if that's what they want. But for them, too, it is advisable to consider one's own proposition and come up with a vision of the new structure. After all, that's what the 'guests' want.

Tourism is becoming an evermore important economic motor for employment and prosperity. In Amsterdam, some 70,000 people work in tourism. The network economy is not only technical but also physical. People travel more and look for new experiences. The Internet and the real-world influence one another; the network economy and the individualisation in society are parallel developments, both influencing one another. Hotels are hindered not only by Airbnb but also by booking sites such as Booking.com and Trivago. If hotels use these sites for reservations, they have to pay a fee; it becomes increasingly difficult to compete independently. However, competition is actually possible on a platform such as Booking.com. Here the supply is presented on the basis of search criteria entered by the customers. For hotels it all comes down to being able to offer something distinctive. For this service, i.e., mediation and marketing, you have to pay a margin, but you do get (many more) customers as a result. The platform in effect becomes the 'market'. You compete on the platform, not with the platform. Platforms acquire a dominant market position, but within the platform, the competition between the suppliers is open.

The following are just a few examples of developments that are possible due to the network economy:

- bundling supply;
- facilitating interactivity;
- taking advantage of the technological possibilities.

Particularly the strength of the so-called multisided platforms, which mediate between supply and demand on the basis of needs, ensures for different competitive relationships. These occur on a global scale where local markets are connected directly, not on the basis of geography but on the basis of users, suppliers or customers. It used to be inconceivable that local shops would have to compete with shops in America or China or that we would be able to have direct contact with our friends anywhere in the world, and even be able to have direct visual communication with them through various types of video-streaming services.

A platform is a collaboration between parties, and the various types of platforms are as follows:

- demand-driven platforms, the mediator between demand and supply;
- aggregators (the bundling of supply) whose aim is to sell on behalf of various parties;
- information platforms whose aim is to provide specific objective answers to questions (for example, regarding science, health or tourist information);
- communication platforms that set up the communication between visitors, for example Facebook, as well as video platforms such as YouTube.

In a platform business model, value is created by the owner of the platform as an independent intermediary, by matching two (or more) mutually dependent parties, as well as connecting them and facilitating the direct interaction between these parties.

This network economy forms the basis for many changes. Some changes, such as the above-mentioned platforms, can already be seen and are leading to disruption in markets. Other applications have just been introduced or are yet to be introduced (such as blockchain). These will have a disruptive impact, but what can you do as a traditional supplier? Nothing, change or join other successful parties? The forces involved are quite considerable — from suppliers in Silicon Valley with plenty of money to consumers who adopt quickly. The decision is actually taken for you, with the market leaders becoming more dominant than they ever were. We can see the end of competition in its traditional form. But is that a bad thing? Are the advantages of traditional competition such that it should be maintained or will competition take place at other levels and in different ways? Old legislation from another era stands in the way of progress. Perhaps it is a good idea to see what has happened in the past and to examine the greatest drives behind the changes.

How Did We Get Here?

Traditional society is based on an analogue approach, often on physical principles. Society has changed slowly, and only major shocks have had any impact on the circumstances. Wars (such as the Second World War) have led to changes, but it is particularly the application of technology that has resulted in major societal changes. Technological developments continued to form the basis for not only change but also the foundation for economic growth, efficiency in the production process and international trade.

The First Industrial Revolution[1] in the 18th century, with the steam engine and mechanisation, resulted in the emergence of factories and subsequent major social demographic changes. The infrastructure was adapted, too, in order to enable train traffic (initially in England). The agricultural society changed, with many *nouveau riche* emerging (factory owners) as well as new dependants (the workers). This divergence led to undesirable situations such as poverty and dependency. The largest motors behind this change were transport, logistics and machinery (first powered by water and then later steam). International trade started to flourish (with England leading the way), and the technological foundation (factories) ensured for a more efficient production process and growth (albeit limited) of prosperity. This prosperity was, however, unfortunately not evenly distributed among the various population groups.

The most important changes were as follows:

- machines substituting manpower (e.g., for textiles);
- new forms of power production (e.g., waterpower, steam engines);
- use and processing of new materials in different ways (such as cotton and linen).

The Second Industrial Revolution started at the end of the 19th century, with the application of technology in new forms of transport: the car and the airplane. The world consequently became smaller and the physical infrastructure was modified again, with roads alongside railways. Technological changes in turn led to a chain reaction and to changes in society. The introduction of electricity around the turn-of-the-century, i.e., from the late 19th to the early 20th century, also resulted in a disruptive change. 'The end of night' became a reality, increasing the length of days and making new developments possible. The new inventions

---

[1] Read, for example, Freeman, Joshua B. (2018). *Behemoth: A History of the Factory and the Making of the Modern World*, Norton & Company, New York.

that arose from this, such as the telegraph and telephone, made the world even smaller and led to new forms of communication. First the newspapers were published; this was quickly followed by the invention of the radio.

The motors of change were the technologies (which sped up and improved mobility), the distribution of information and new forms of communication. International trade became evermore important and prosperity increased. America led the way, while the new discoveries resulted in further prosperity and a new elite (the owners of the machines).

The most important changes were as follows:

- a broader impact of technology on society;
- the application of the combustion engine (cars, aviation, machinery);
- mass production through further industrialisation and applications in the processing industry.

The Third Industrial Revolution started in the 1960s with the emergence and application of computers. These computers initially had a facilitative function and enabled greater efficiency by taking over certain tasks; manual work became automated. The areas in which the computers were applied changed particularly in the 1970s and the decades that followed. Automation increasingly developed into computerisation (information technology (IT)), making information more accessible and improving the communication medium. This development heralded the disruptive changes that were in store for many facets of our daily lives. It also meant the start of the service sector. Due to the increased computerisation, the decision-making process became evermore complex, leading to the creation of more services that would help and relieve companies and individuals in this work. Services were developed that would help to interpret the information to allow for better decisions. Although these changes did lead to adaptations, the old structures remained intact in many cases. **Changes require time, acceptance and vision**.

All three factors (computerisation, communication and efficiency applications) needed time, but small changes had major consequences.[2]

---

[2]The computer service company RAET in Arnhem was initially part of Heidemaatschappij (1965) before it became independent. The name stood for Computer Centre for Administration, Efficiency and Technology.

IT helped in gaining greater knowledge and insight into what was happening, and the mobility broadened the perspectives of private individuals, businesses and leaders. Old boundaries (mental and physical) came under pressure. There were also major consequences on the political front. The Eastern bloc could not hold up, and the wall fell. China (Asia) emerged as a world power and America profited maximally from its head start (America did not suffer any economic damage from the Second World War; this actually resulted in an economic revival with America becoming the world leader). Increasingly more capital became available for investments, a reinforcing process, which led to greater prosperity and new applications in the area of technology. The emergence of the Internet as an information and communication medium, in the early 1990s, was the last step in a change process from limits (restrictive) to no limits. Physical limitations became virtual challenges. In the Netherlands, the rank and file of the political parties continued to remain faithful to this for quite some time. It was only at the start of the 21st century that the old electoral structure was breached, in particular by the new 18-year-old (and older) electorate.

America became increasingly important as a world leader and undisputedly led the way when it came to technology. Companies such as GE (General Electric) and IBM, as well as the automobile industry and particularly large companies in the telecommunication and automation sectors, developed a new infrastructure that was led by America. This was considerably more extensive and far-reaching than ever before and affected all facets of daily life. Due to this development, the American lifestyle became the norm, and American prosperity the aspiration.

The most important changes are as follows:

- the use of computer technology in industry and in durable and consumable products;
- mass production and marketing for mass markets;
- greater efficiency and increased internationalisation.

We now hear about the Fourth Industrial Revolution based on Internet applications. Barriers of time, location, information, timeliness and communication are disappearing rapidly. These developments are leading to changes, often disruptions, and are no longer limited to a particular area. They are *interconnected*. The applications and changes in a geographical area, in society or in the applications of the technology are *interchangeable*. They can be applied directly in many areas. It is no longer possible to isolate a particular application (whether per application area or geographical area). Thanks to the Internet, everything is interconnected, and there is insight into the consequences and the possibilities of changes. The accessibility of information is helping to empower everyone more than ever before. Knowledge and power are being devolved to anyone who wants it. This is the basis of the network economy. The development from an agricultural society to an industrial society, then to a society based on IT, will eventually lead to a network economy that connects everything with everyone. This Fourth Industrial Revolution is much more far-reaching than all other previous industrial revolutions. The rules of play will have to be discovered and determined all over again. This period of transformation will of course lead to frictions, tensions and new balances of power (Figure 1).

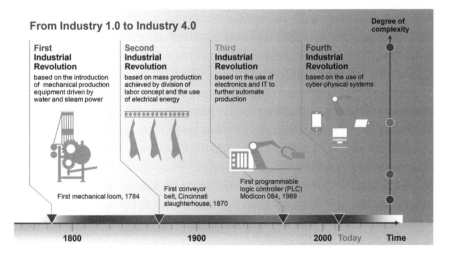

Figure 1.   From Industry 1.0 to Industry 4.0 (engineersjournal.com).

Important changes are the following:

- unparalleled speed and extent of the changes;
- disruption of all markets and industries, as well as consumer behaviour;
- a structural change of systems, production, society and markets.

What has the Past Taught Us?

The first two industrial revolutions were primarily focused on the transition from human production capacity to machine production capacity, as well as on the automation and optimisation of processes. During the Third Industrial Revolution, the emerging possibilities of IT and electronics made a shift possible from a (mass) focus on products to a focus on product adaptations for a particular target group. This allowed more individualised options to be offered that could meet a specific demand. The Fourth Industrial Revolution makes use of the ubiquitous availability of data and communication, which allows customers (and consumers) full control of the production processes.

The customers and consumers are able to remotely control the production processes by sending data that are based on their individual wishes. In this way, a customer-oriented (specific) product can be generated in a series with a batch size of one.

- The old rules of competition were based on the old structures, the application of which is now an outdated technology.
- It is a battle between 'doing digital', whereby traditional processes are made more efficient through digital possibilities, and 'being digital', whereby the technology forms the basis for new structures and applications.
- The new businesses mentioned earlier are based on digital technology and make optimal use of the new possibilities of the network economy.
- It is a battle between traditional structures and new structures, a battle between old technological applications and new possibilities. This is similar to the battle we saw in the past between swords and gunpowder, between the horse and the train, then later the bicycle and the car.

- The old structures and technologies will increasingly lose strength and power. But what are the new structures and competitive relationships?

The changes to traditional systems, whereby the customers lead the way, are happening on the basis of these insights. Old physical boundaries are disappearing due to the possibilities offered by networks. A worldwide market is being created where businesses have to compete and customers are able to buy. You could compare this to a site that was initially enclosed by a fence, with a locked gate. Suddenly the lock disappeared, then the gate, and eventually the fence. The site is now freely accessible and merged with the surrounding area. So why would visitors still come to this particular site?

Join In or Wait?

The old structures are stubborn, as the old decision-makers continue to hold on to them. Often, the knowledge to identify the consequences of new developments and respond to them is unavailable. Although online sales have been growing in double figures year-on-year for the last two decades, retailers and interest groups have refused to recognise the impact on the shops on the high street. In addition, others look for other causes for the problems in the retail sector: the recession, increased mobility. The true causes of the changes, however, were not recognised.

- The new Internet-based applications, such as webshops, smartphones and a different buying behaviour, were dismissed for too long.
- Reduced budgets and young people having other choices led to a different buying behaviour and decreased expenditure on physical products in particular.
- It was only once the number of empty shop premises in shopping centres reached a certain point that action was taken, but mainly within traditional structures without really responding to the different choices and buying behaviour. External factors continued being blamed. In other words, there is nothing we can do about it!

First of all, the old structures were made more efficient, such as lower parking costs, longer shop opening hours, Sunday openings and lower prices. In the Dutch town of Drachten, shops are allowed to stay open 24/7 in response to online sales. This is incredibly naive.

This initial drive towards efficiency is typical for traditional decision-makers. The decisions could then, after all, be made within one's own comfort zone. The customers' buying behaviour, new technology and the unpredictable behaviour of the younger generation lead to uncertainty. But ignoring the changes gives peace of mind. And this can be seen outside the retail sector as well. It is evident in every link of the production and marketing chain. Traditional structures are modified, but not changed.

Do One's Own Restrictions Lead to a Tunnel Vision in the Decision-Making?

Manufacturers are able to supply their goods directly, without calling upon further links in the chain, but are afraid of the consequences. The aggrieved links in the chain might perhaps retaliate by no longer selling or recommending the products (short-term consequences). The power in the chain holds back the changes through fear. That is, until other providers come along, often from other markets or from abroad, who do sell directly, often at lower prices and with services that appeal to the buyer (24/7, return guarantee). Then finally action is taken, and hopefully on time. But the many bankruptcies and takeovers give pause for concern. So how does it get to this situation? It is, of course, to do with this fear of leaving one's comfort zone, as well as the fear of the consequences of change to the traditional structure. But it can also be due to a reluctance to act or the strict conditions of doing business such as profitability level, stock market prices or company bonuses.

But there are also other principles that come to play here, such as the consensus approach (trying to keep everyone happy, consensus decision-making being typical in the Netherlands), as well as one's own knowledge and approach as we will see later (applying what we have learned during our studies and deciding on the basis of our own experience). Traditional businesses and decision-makers are stuck to the constraints of the past which slows down decision-making. When making decisions, one calls upon one's personal knowledge and experience, while the developments simply continue. In addition, information is usually interpreted from the perspective of one's own field of expertise or vision (no lateral thinking). For a long time, I kept on hearing that Amazon was not a threat; it was, after all, not making any profit. This reveals a complete lack of knowledge of Amazon's business model, which was not based upon short-term profitability, but on long-term value creation. And the same can be said for Bol.com. As far as these naive decision-makers were concerned, it was not necessary to study the developments, nor to take any action, as these new entrants would not last long.

Are the Old (Physical) Structures too Oppressive?

Another problem with change is the traditional structure. Companies continue to rely upon fixed structures, structures that arose within stable markets. Many continue to hold on to the traditional decisions of the supply chain and the decision that every supplier and company has to be an independent entity. This leads to control and less dependence, more certainty therefore. Suppliers (the independent entities) compete with one another for the best proposition for the customer, consumer or business. They often still use the traditional marketing instruments: Product, Place, Promotion and Price, with competition mainly being based on price, while that says nothing about the usability, quality or value within a production process. On the Internet, price is transparent, making price comparisons easy. But do people actually buy just on the basis of price? There is the perception that a low price is always beneficial for the buyer! In the old model, pricing has always been a dominant competitive weapon. In the 1980s, Michael Porter based his competitive strategies on the traditional market structure and the mutual competition between suppliers.

Old competition models were based on the following traditional structures:

- greater competitive strength through more efficient processes (the value chain);
- greater competitive strength through a focus on other suppliers in the market;
- by protecting the market as much as possible.

However, in the last decade there has been a growing realisation that there is an actual value proposition and that a sale involves an exchange of values of which price is only one component.

Control is important within the old structures. Among independent entities, control is often linked to possession and/or ownership. A company has its own premises, factories, machines, fleet of vehicles, staff with permanent contracts and a management board that does not change often. Supervisory boards are often old decision-makers with years of experience with the old structure. The capital of such a company can be personal capital (such as with a PLC), and also borrowed capital (loans) or the property of an investor who has more of a short-term vision (private equity). Interest is paid on this and investors tend to be more focused on the profits (efficiency). This short-term approach is a typical Anglo-Saxon approach to business. Porter's value chain (1985) shows the total value of the value chain and consists of the organisation's primary and secondary value activities as well as a margin.

Primary value activities are directly related to the physical creation, sale, supply and servicing of a company's product or service. The competition is based on the old instruments of price, product, place and promotion.

- *Inbound logistics*: This refers to all activities related to the receipt, storage and distribution of purchased materials and/or services that are used in the production process of the company. The supplier partnerships play an important part in the creation of value.
- *Operations*: This denotes to all activities that have to do with converting this input into the final product for the customer and include processing, packaging and assembly.
- *Outbound logistics*: These activities relate to the supply of a product and/or service to the customer and include aspects such as an organisation's collection, storage and distribution systems.
- *Marketing*: This includes all activities that stimulate the buyer to enter into a transaction, which include advertising, promotion and price.
- *Sales*: This indicates all activities that ensure that the buyers are able to purchase the product, which include channel selection and the customer relations with these channels.

- *Service*: This represents all activities that are concerned with delivering service in order to increase or maintain the value of the product and/service. Examples include installation, repair, advice and delivery of parts.

The following secondary activities support the above-mentioned primary functions:

- *Procurement*: This refers to the function of purchasing materials and/or services that are used in the production process of the company. This therefore does not refer to the purchased *inputs* themselves. This includes finding suppliers and negotiating the best price.
- *Human resource management*: This refers to all the activities that relate to recruiting, hiring, training, developing, motivating, remunerating and retaining the staff necessary to carry out the value activities.
- *Technological development*: This indicates all the activities related to managing and processing information as well as protecting the knowledge base of a company.
- *Firm infrastructure*: This consists of the functions that allow a company to carry out its daily activities such as accounting, legal matters, administration and general management.

The margin is the difference between the total value and the costs for carrying out the value activities in a linear sequence of the value chain.

What are the New Value Activities in the Competitive Battle?

In order to determine where the value activities and margin are located in a platform (network) company, you first have to look at how the essential capitals in a platform business model (infrastructure, network and data) are related to one another. The study carried out by Choudary (2015) revealed three different types of architectural layers that were repeatedly found in all the types of platforms. Figure 2 shows the three layers of platforms.

Figure 2.   Architectural layers of platforms (Choudary, 2015).

Choudary (2015) suggests that the external network of producers adds value to the network layer. In order to make this value creation possible, however, platforms require a second layer: infrastructure. This layer comprises the tools, services and rules that make interaction in a multisided market possible. This layer has little value in itself, unless users create value in the platform. All platforms use data because the information helps the platform to gear the supply to the demand. The data layer creates relevancy and matches the most relevant content, product and/or services with the appropriate users.

It's important to first build the infrastructure in order to make interactions in the above-mentioned layer possible. As manufacturers and consumers adopt the infrastructure, an ecosystem begins to evolve. This becomes the next observable phase in the evolution of the platform. And finally, the interaction between manufacturers and consumers on the platform generates huge amounts of data. The data layer then helps to make future interactions more efficient and keeps users regularly engaged with the platform. The use of data from the data layer has a positive effect on the value perception of users in the network layer (Choudary, 2015).

What are the Sources of Value Creation?

1. The focus is shifting towards the demand side of the economy (Van Alstyne *et al.*, 2016). This can be found on the right-hand side of the traditional value chain.
2. In a platform business model, products and/or services are not actually produced; the organisation does not organise its production processes, and as a result there is no control over the creation of value within the production process. Value is brought in by external producers, so the production process disappears as an activity from a platform company's value chain.

3. As platforms have different groups of users on all sides, the value creation moves from left to right and from right to left. This change in the value chain is an important characteristic of a two-sided market. There is therefore no longer a value chain with value activities that take place in a linear sequence, and the consumer is no longer located at the end of these processes but forms part of the value creation within a value network.

Primary Activities and Platform Companies

The platform business model is not aimed at the physical creation, sales, supply and service of a company's own product or service. This results in the value activities of inbound logistics, operations and outbound logistics disappearing from the value chain and the direct control of the platform company.

The owner of the platform creates value as an independent intermediary, by matching and connecting two (or more) mutually dependent parties with one another and facilitating the direct interaction between these parties (Eisenmann *et al.*, 2006; Osterwalder and Pigneur, 2010). The aim of marketing here is no longer to bring about a transaction for a company's product and/or service but to realise a value exchange between supply and demand.

The most important capital of a platform company for providing this value proposition consists of the following:

- an infrastructure for direct interaction (the platform);
- the presence of network effects that arise when two (or more) sides of the market have an interdependence, supply and demand, resulting in the growth of the network;
- the availability of data arising from the interaction via the platform, thereby creating matching functionalities and the relevance of the platform.

The most important value activities can thus be described as platform management, platform promotion and service provision to the network (Osterwalder and Pigneur, 2010).

Secondary Activities and Platform Companies

The traditional organisational structures are still preventing most companies from looking for talented staff outside the boundaries of their organisation. This makes it difficult for companies to tackle evermore complex challenges. Many platform companies allow people outside their payroll to offer their expertise in new ways. Network organisations concentrate on orchestrating tasks rather than on the 'ownership' of full-time workers. Whereas Marriott hotel employs large numbers of staff to realise its value proposition of 'accommodation for a guest', Airbnb uses external hosts to provide the same value proposition. Human Resource Management shifts, as a result, more and more towards community management (Choudary, 2015).

Technological development is evidently no longer a supporting activity, but is essential in the optimisation of the platform and its functions. Platform companies still have other supporting tasks but these are increasingly losing relevance.

Shouldn't Investments be Made with a Long-Term Vision?

Traditional companies are mature, often having grown during the second and third industrial age, whereby ownership, control, independence and supply chains were important. If these companies are taken over, it is often due to profit and returns. Private equity groups want to make the companies more efficient and effective, and then sell them off entirely or piecemeal, at a profit.

In some cases, the company profits are reinvested if this leads to an increase in value (therefore higher returns in the sale). Sometimes the company profits are creamed off by charging the investment to the company, which then has to pay interest on this (or perhaps even pay off this debt). Whatever the case may be, these investors use their expertise to realise a return on their investment through greater efficiency and increased value. If the scope to realise this is longer than four years, these investors start to feel uneasy as they would prefer to invest in new promising objects, anywhere in the world.

The investors involved in the new start-ups are not interested in short-term profits. They believe in the great opportunities for growth of these companies and are convinced that a long-term investment would provide better results. What's more, they are often investors who have already made an investment and successfully divested it (often through a stock market flotation, a so-called IPO). As a result, they have substantial investment portfolios. Quickly selling the company again (with profit) would only lead to the problem of looking for another promising project. Staying put and growing along with the traditional project is therefore a better option. These new entrants have a longer term commitment and vision, which results in more stable and lasting growth. At investment level, there is a conflict between the traditional companies that are focused more on profits and the new companies that are looking to increase value (through growth). The new investors are focused more on the long-term effects. What's more, the new companies only have a short history and limited 'legacy', as a result of which they can straightaway use the latest technologies. The management are creative, flexible and often young leaders who respond more quickly and in an unorthodox manner to the market conditions and buying behaviour. The growth of these new companies is partly at the expense of the more traditional companies. This is typically a friction in a transformation period (from the Third to the Fourth Industrial Revolution).

Many start-ups have emerged in America. The conditions for this were clear and were as follows:

- a concentrated area where the developments took place (Silicon Valley); this provided a concentrated supply of good personnel, as well as a concentration of investors who were keen on investing in new technological companies based on a long-term vision;
- a large home market that enabled testing among a relatively large group, thereby not risking any further damage in the market should the start-up fail;
- a good business climate where success is appreciated and failure (bankruptcy) is accepted;
- a competitive business climate.

On top of this, America had come out of the Second World War unscathed. The war production actually helped to initiate strong economic growth, making America the world leader. As a result, it gained a head start on many other countries that had to build up their economies once more and where spending power of companies and families had to return once again.

The Growth of the Network Economy, Technology or Human Behaviour?

China and America benefit from a growing network economy. This will lead to new prosperity and employment as well as connections on a global scale. This development not only is facilitated by the technology but also needs to be accepted (and adopted) by companies, governments and consumers. This network economy has to form part of the changes that are taking place in the behaviour of consumers and companies.

Technology facilitates and stimulates this development

Technology facilitates change. Technology was initially used in developments to realise greater efficiency, but these days technology is used much more often for connection and communication purposes. Technology is also used to carry out analyses, which helps to bring about a better bond between users and suppliers (commitment and loyalty).

- New methods, such as scrum and micro-services, ensure for a speedy development.
- Modifications of systems, other applications, are based on network facilities.
- The cloud ensures that everyone has access to the desired data at any time and place and that everyone can communicate regardless of where they are.

Although the application of these technological developments has been growing for decades now, it is only in the last few years that we can speak of a convergence, where developments are influencing one another. Both the application and the acceptance have greatly accelerated, in part of course due to the technological possibilities, partly through the economic necessity particularly of China and America and due to the global acceptance by companies and individuals as well.

Products were increasingly no longer made specifically by one single factory; rather, production involved the assembly of various components to form a single product. This not only greatly reinforced the mutual dependency involved in the production but also stimulated specialisation. From a legal point of view, a factory was still an independent entity, but not necessarily when it came to its activities. A factory would sometimes receive semi-manufactured goods, which would then have to be processed further and then sent elsewhere in the world to be finished off and sold to a particular market. This network manufacturing process is also supported by information and communication. Each link in this process is independent yet connected with another link for further processing. And so a chain of independent units, nodes, is created that together formed a single entity. This is the basis for the network economy (Figure 3).

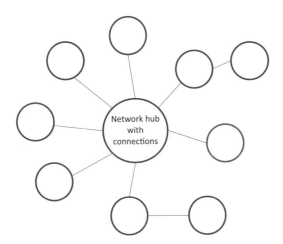

Figure 3.   The network structure, independent entities (nodes) are connected.[3]

---

[3]In telecommunication networks, a node is a junction, a redistribution point or a communication end point. The definition of a junction depends on the network and the protocol level to which it refers.

The buying behaviour (consumers and companies) is changing

A second development is based on the behaviour of buyers. The behaviour is increasingly individual, and consumers are becoming more assertive and better informed. What's more, thanks to the Internet everyone has access to sources of information and communication. The penetration of smartphones is above 80% in all age groups. In addition, the old purchasing barrier to online shopping no longer exists; it is just as easy to buy in one's own country as it is abroad. The disadvantages of not being able to see and touch the product and having to wait for delivery are accepted because of the many advantages, such as access to all the desired information, a wide choice on the Internet, price transparency, the right to return items and home delivery. Target groups, a distinctive feature since the 1960s (the Third Industrial Revolution), are rapidly disappearing due to individualisation. A consequence of this is the demand-driven approach aimed at the individual buyer, which contributes to the individual buying behaviour.

Social economic changes

And finally, there are also socio-economic aspects to this change, which contribute to the rapid growth of the network economy: increased prosperity, the large rise in single-parent families and singles and the choices made by young people (millennials) that are increasingly based on well-being rather than on prosperity. This individual behaviour is determined by the individual wishes and circumstances. Furthermore, this new generation has grown up in prosperity, with technology and has very good communication skills. The focus on oneself rather than on a group has also contributed to this.

Adjusting to international developments

For many years, governments have sought to remove trade restrictions. Bilateral and multilateral trade agreements, close collaborations between countries (such as within the European Union, and the European Union with other countries), have led to an increase in global trade and prosperity. The first step, removing barriers, had been taken, but within the old structures (product-based). The second step, as a result of the changing competitive position in the markets, quickly followed. Companies had to meet international norms and international competition conditions. This meant that companies started to strive for both quality improvements and efficiency.

By responding to these changes and applying new possibilities, opportunities for new business models arose. New communities have been created (such as social networks) where like-minded people can find one another. But this has also led to frictions in companies, which suddenly have to become part of a network, which causes major changes to competitive relationships. This requires changes to a company's business model, to the organisation and to the company's focus. Organisations are no longer those independent entities working in a stable and predictable market. The market has become difficult to predict and the changes require constant monitoring and adaptation. Dynamism and speed of change are essential in order to be able to compete in the network economy. This requires not only flexibility from an organisation but also the appropriate expertise and skills.

Building Blocks for the Future

- Traditional structures restrict the application of new possibilities.
- New applications of technology not only lead to collaboration within a network but also create different competitive relationships.
- Organisations as independent entities have to join a partnership within a network.
- In addition to the technological changes, it is the acceptance of users, customers and companies that form the basis for disruption.
- The playing field is no longer limited to a traditional target group or protected market. Competition is now global. Purchases are demand-driven. The demand economy is replacing the supply model.
- Competition takes place on the basis of algorithms that often lack transparency.

The traditional platform development is disrupting traditional competitive relationships in a number of ways as follows:

- It reduces barriers to access.
- Everyone can start a new platform. Alternatively, a company can become a member of a platform.
- There is a change in the logic of value creation and value determination.
- The platforms provide a new series of economic relationships, which are dependent upon the Internet (networks). This leads to an ecosystem that is the basis of value creation. The ecosystem determines the conditions users need to meet in order to participate.
- Value is determined by a variety of mechanisms, each of which has different implications for the distribution of profits. Platforms transform the work and the relationships or create new categories of work and relationships.
- It regulates the relationships and provides arbitration in the event of disputes.
- This means that the platform can be used for arbitration without breaking the law.
- Small group of businesses and investors work for the platform; it is they who take the risk. They earn very well from this and, if the business is successful, will profit from the value that is activated on the (stock) market.
- Then there are also (small) companies that deliver goods for the platform. They are in fact mini-operators or consignees. Most of these will not be successful or profitable, though some will be very successful.
- There will be a number of employment relationships that involve long hours at the office and benefits such as healthcare, but most such relationships will be defined anew, resulting in the creation of jobs with very flexible hours but fewer of the traditional benefits. In the food delivery sector, there will be a large increase in the demand for food deliverers, boys and girls, to deliver these meals. In addition, possibly even a greater demand for cooks to prepare these meals. The deliverers are usually able to choose their own hours, and therefore work very flexible hours, but are hired mainly as freelancers and so do not enjoy

many of the traditional employment conditions. We see this not only within food delivery companies but also clearly within transport companies (Uber) and parcel delivery services (post.nl).

- Repositioning of power in the economic system will happen.
- The manager or owner of a platform varies per platform. The differences are important as the distribution of the benefits varies per owner of the platform. Platforms such as Foodora and Deliveroo are a third party, but there are also restaurants that have started their own platforms for delivering meals. In such cases where a third party owns a platform, the restaurant benefits from more business. If the restaurant has its own platform, then the restaurant enjoys more commercial benefits as well as the advantage of customers loyal to the platform (Zysman and Kenney, 2016).

Bibliography

Choudary, S. P. (2018). *The Architecture of Digital Labour Platforms: Policy Recommendations on Platform Design for Worker Well-Being.* International Labour Office, Geneva.

Eisenmann, T., Parker, G., Van Alstyne, M. (October 2006). Strategies for two-sided markets, *Harvard Business Review* 84(10): 92–101.

Osterwalder, A. and Pigneur, Y. (2010). *Business Model Generation: A Handbook for Visionaries, Game Changers, and Challengers.* Wiley, New Jersey.

Porter, M. E. (1985). *Competitive Advantage: Creating and Sustaining Superior Performance.* Free Press, New York, 557 p.

Van Alstyne, M. W., Parker, G., and Choudary, S. P. (2016). Pipelines, platforms, and the new rules of strategy, *Harvard Business Review*, April.

Zysman, J. and Kenney, M. (2016). *The Next Phase in the Digital Revolution Platforms, Abundant Computing, Growth and Employment*, 17 October 2016.

Chapter 3

The New Market Conditions*

The use of the Internet has changed the competitive relationships and the market conditions. As a result, it has become necessary for providers to go along with the innovation of one of the providers. When a provider successfully applies new technologies within the traditional business model, it can lead to lower costs in the so-called input–output model and in the processing. The application of the Internet can consequently reduce the price level or, if the market price forms the basis, lead to a higher profit margin. Other providers would have to tag along to ensure they do not fall behind the competition. This is a vicious circle; despite the innovation brought about by the Internet, this will only lead to an increasingly level playing field.

Do the Traditional Competition Models Restrict Innovation?

The old view that a business makes products and then sells them within the supply chain is no longer so relevant. Certainly not for the so-called

---

*This chapter has in part used research by Tim Scholtes and Jan Biezepol, eMarketing students at RSM/Erasmus University.

non-daily products and for applications within the business-to-business (B2B) market. (Say's law: supply creates its own demand, should actually be: demand creates its own supply.) Thanks to the enormous knowledge and information that purchasing parties can access, they can be much more selective in their purchasing decisions. Organisations should no longer have a sales focus but a purchasing focus. They should no longer first produce a product and then try to find a market for it. They should instead start with the customer: what do they want, who are they, how have they changed and what motivates their decisions. This shift from a production orientation to a customer orientation results in the following:

- companies that gear products better to the needs of (often individual) customers;
- greater satisfaction;
- the creation of loyalty;
- a more concentrated strategy for businesses.

I will take a closer look at this customer focus when I later analyse the model of Treacy and Wiersema as well as during the assessment of various models.

Porter observes the market and product-related factors. He looks at, for example, the availability of replacement products, but does not ask himself whether these products lead to the same loyalty with consumers (customers). Nor whether preferences in the future will change, allowing a company to prepare for this change (just look at the examples of both Kodak and Nokia). This is actually the general criticism levelled at Porter's model as well as other competition models that are based on the supply. In the traditional market, which is very dynamic and characterised by a dynamic demand, different conditions apply. Companies should take advantage of the opportunities available, but they are constantly on the defensive. This results in a less effective strategy. There are plenty of examples of this strong focus on products and traditional markets, such as Kodak, Nokia, retailers on the high street and travel agencies. The traditional strength of companies is collaboration in a network based on one's own added value. A purchase/customer focus based on engagement requires a different type of strategy (customer-oriented), a different type of organisation (agile, flexible) and a different supply proposition and value exchange (based on customer needs). By now focusing on increasing their value, companies have to dispose of divisions that do not contribute to this. Traditional outdated competition models, which are still based on supply, stand in the way of innovation and change. If companies continue to hang on to those competition models for too long, they will quickly fall behind the competition and find themselves separated from the new entrants by a chasm that will be impossible to bridge.

Will the Rivalry between Providers (Competitors) Change?

The first modification I would like to make relates to the 'Rivalry between traditional competitors'. This component is best suited to a product-oriented supply chain, aimed at defending market share. Competition has always been regarded as something negative, while these days we see collaboration with competitors based on added value. One should not look at who is a competitor and how a company can compete against them. Rather, one should look at whether there is an opportunity for collaboration and creating value in a network. Instead of only looking at the extent and strength of the competitors, it is better to keep an eye on their willingness to work together. And to see if there are any traditional relationships that can be used, any historical behaviour with regard to working together. Collaborative partnerships, resulting in complete supply chain ecosystems are the central element of modern supply chains. In actual fact, the basis of competition is not to defeat the competition but to motivate customers (Table 1).

So What is the New Supply Chain Then?

The traditional supply chain involved a linear process, where successive links added value. Each link was independent, and had its own revenue model and position. The totality of these independent links was the supply chain. Information was passed on from link to link. As a result, factories

Table 1.   Overview of value creation, old and new.

Porter's Five Forces Model	Traditional	Network Based
Substitute of products	Competing on the basis of quality and experience.	Ensuring there is a powerful network with complementary products and suppliers.
Entrants	Erecting barriers based on local position, price, speedy deliveries, distribution and presence.	Ensuring there is added value and possible balloting for new entrants. Providing customer loyalty.
Negotiating power of supplier	Limited number of providers, with attention on the competitors and a distinctive supply.	Choices based on needs and wishes. Price is only one component.
Negotiating power of customers	Ensuring there is a unique product, effective distribution channel with limited negotiation freedom (for example, prices).	Based on needs and wishes. Customer provides a basis for matching.
Rivalry in the market	Market position and market share form the basis. A clear focus on other providers/competitors.	Via the network but based on the filtering in the matching module.

had limited information regarding customers, buying processes and buying motives. The customers of a manufacturer were the companies of the next link in the chain, not the end customer. This was typical for the traditional analogue approach, but was a major limitation if you needed to respond to a dynamic market.

By using networks, platforms, a totally different model arises: the supply chain ecosystem. Here, all parties work together in a network that forms dynamically. Each collaboration is different, but in all cases the information is shared. This is typical for a platform where a match develops between providers and consumers. There is a much greater understanding of the buying motives and customer preferences. Certain links in the chain even become redundant as the function is taken over by other parties. Are shops still needed if manufacturers and wholesalers can supply customers directly? Platforms and networks lead to a *disintermediation,* or implosion, of a supply chain. Each party has to determine its added value in the ecosystem all over again. Information leads to transparency, so there is a better response to the demand. As a result of this transparency, as well as the direct relationship, customers are better able to gear the demand to the supply. In addition, the costs associated with an ecosystem, the network, will be lower than in a linear supply chain. There are, after all, fewer parties involved, and therefore fewer costs and lucrative links. The final price will consequently be lower or better attuned to the dynamics in the market. *Dynamic pricing* is an example of this: a price that depends on customer demand.

Should You be Afraid of Newcomers?

If the basic principles of rivalry change then the fear for newcomers will also change. The true competitive strength lies in the power of one's own network: the providers, the customers and knowledge of the search and buying processes. In addition, a high degree of engagement also leads to a decreasing switch behaviour. Newcomers should be assessed on the basis of added value. Collaboration could lead to a reinforcement of the network and the pushing back of boundaries both physical and in terms of the supply and other forms of collaboration. In this way, the threat is turned into an opportunity for collaboration and cross-industrial partnerships, with a view to creating an ecosystem (network) and an accurate picture of the appeal and possibilities of new market conditions. We see this in, for example, the automobile industry, where sometimes more than 20 manufacturers collaborate in the production of a single car. This collaboration can also be seen in the platform economy where various parties work together towards the final product or for the end consumer; also in logistics, production, as well as distributors and possibly other suppliers offering add-on products. Competition no longer takes place on the basis of product features, but on customer bonding, the community. New entrants therefore have to win over customers from a traditional community to their own community. The greater the bonding with customers and the stronger the relationship with them, the harder it is for newcomers to prise customers away from the current providers. The competitive strength is therefore determined by the strength of the network.

Can Existing Products be Threatened by Replacement Products or Services?

Increasingly, more providers changed their products on the basis of the wishes of the user, thereby creating new products and services that competed with the old products and services. Examples include Nokia, which allowed its mobile phone to remain solely a telephone, while Apple turned its phone into a computer with Internet access. Restaurants offered meals in the restaurant itself or as a takeaway option, while Thuisbezorgd offered to bring meals to the home. Webshops enabled customers to order online and try out the product at home, while the shops on the high street clung onto their physical locations and limited opening hours. E-Bikes changed the options people had regarding bicycles, thereby offering possibilities to new entrants such as Stella. Traditional providers remained sluggish and were slow to make changes to their distribution model (via dealers), while customers started to buy more online (fietsenwinkel.nl), or the shop actually came to the customers (as with Stella). In many cases, traditional providers were too late in identifying the threat posed by substitute products and services. In the old sales model too little account is taken of the buying elements of the product (sales arguments must change to purchase arguments).

These buying arguments comprise the physical product, the services and perception. This used to be regarded as a single entity, whereby one party (the manufacturer) supplied the product and usually ensured there was a positive perception with a product guarantee and advertising for the product (brands). The shop/dealer took care of the delivery, along with some extra services. This is the strength of a dealer/shop in the linear supply chain. Due to the role of the Internet in the buying process (both with webshops and platforms as well as through searches) these days it provides the information that allows customers to become more assertive, while webshops offer services that regular shops cannot provide. As a result, a shop has become merely a distribution point for products. The costs of the physical location, however, are too high. This creates unequal competition with on the one hand manufacturers, who started to supply directly (via a platform, an aggregator, such as Bol.com or Amazon.com or a Multi-sided platform, an MSP platform), and with webshops on the other hand, which due to the possibility of direct communication have more information on the customers and their buying motives. The physical sales outlets have to figure out their role anew or will disappear.[1]

How will the negotiating power of suppliers change?

In the traditional approach (of Porter) this form of competition was based on established markets and fixed market relationships. Technology led to efficiency; but robotisation also led to equivalent products — the same appearance and same quality. The negotiations were based on prices and margins. Due to the new entrants, with their different focus, keen prices and considerable service, the competitive relationships have changed. The first response involved trying to keep costs down by employing cheaper personnel, increasing efficiency and outsourcing to low-wage countries. These actions did not always lead to success. As the product supply became transparent, the power of the purchaser increased. The number of providers also increased, thanks to the possibilities offered by networks and the Internet.

This collaboration in markets and on platforms is determined by the customer or by providers. The idea behind the MSPs is an integral market approach by various providers (which is why it is described as multisided). A supplier works within the platform together with other, often complementary, parties in order to gain negotiating power and market reach. This is convenient for buyers, as they only have to negotiate with one party. This far-reaching form of collaboration between parties, which characterises the network economy, has a strong influence on the market relationships. Platforms as they are now are the first signs of this. The platform and network become the market; due to the transparency and the analyses, this concept forms a strong competitor for the traditional market relationships and market parties. This changes the chain, but also a supplier's negotiating power (making it stronger and more diverse).

The suppliers' new negotiation position serves as a way of looking at the competition. Traditionally, suppliers look at the competition,

---

[1] See, for example, the analysis in the Dutch newspaper *De Telegraaf* of 16 February 2019.

how many are there and what is their market share; this gives them an indication of the competitive position in the market. It is only possible to observe the competition in the traditional market by looking at what customers are doing (network effects). This is a change that is perfectly in line with the customer-oriented approach of platforms and networks. Buyers and behaviour are central. In this way, it is easy to predict what users will do, as described earlier. The dominant player has an approximately 70% market share, with strong network effects. This reinforces the position of the market leaders and makes people less inclined to switch to a smaller provider. Users trust the platform as well as the providers on the platform. We see this with, for example, Aliexpress.com where customers buy from unknown, usually Chinese, suppliers. Aliexpress.com is the partner that is trusted here.

How will the negotiating power of buyers change?

The next change relates to the 'negotiation power of buyers'. Again, observing how loyal buyers are to a brand based on the market share, the homogeneity of a product and the switching costs, is now outdated. Buyer power is no longer determined by these factors; the switching costs these days are practically zero and products can barely be distinguished from one another. A more accurate measurement of the negotiating power of buyers can be obtained by examining whether there are already strong platforms on the market that make use of strong network effects. Historically, the dominant player in modern markets would acquire a market share of approximately 70%. Network effects therefore determine how successful and large you can become. That is why buyers have, in a certain sense, a much larger responsibility in and effect on the success of companies, through their purchasing and return behaviour. This shows once more the crucial part that buyers play in the traditional market, and shows that the most important goal should be to meet all customer needs.

In all these changes, customers and customer behaviour play an important role in the strength of the network and the competitive relationships. This requires a focus on one's own strong points, as illustrated in the model of Treacy and Wiersema (1995). This focus leads to specialisations and the creation of value, as well as, through the application of the Internet, to lower costs (operational excellence). What is more, there are also the following benefits for the products:

- a stronger market position (product excellence);
- greater distinctiveness through innovation;
- focus leads to greater knowledge of customers and customer behaviour (*customer intimacy*);
- this focus can also lead to a strong position in a niche market.

In a later publication, Fred Wiersema further examines these disciplines and also forms a basis for the traditional network structure.[2] Customers look for certainty and guarantees for the results, not only for products. The suppliers have a value proposition, which provides all those certainties that a buyer desires. The offer is distinguishable from the competition. In the beginning of this century, this was a requirement for providers, whereby products were compared. Now on a platform it is a requirement to make the difference along with all the other providers. A network needs collaboration and teaming in view of the specific focus of each company. This means that there has to be mutual respect between the providers, and by using one another's strengths (values) a much stronger competitive advantage will arise. Mutual trust between the participants and a willingness to work together are important conditions. This also applies to the collaboration with customers; a mutual trust and the certainty that everyone's interests are intertwined.

Wiersema provides a number of guidelines as to how collaboration can be realised in the interest of the customer. The following guidelines also apply to multisided platforms:

- A supplier has to look for partners who want to work together on a solution; a supplier who is concerned with shared interests. This will particularly apply in long-term relationships, such as those in the software industry or with durable products or machines.

---

[2]Wiersema, Fred (2001). *The New Market Leaders.* The Free Press, New York, p. 81, and further examples on pp. 191–192.

- A second focus involves responding to the specific needs and wishes of the customers. Together, providers look for new solutions and new opportunities. This is not only the case with consultants but also with software companies or other services where interaction between the customer and supplier is essential.
- A third focus is the relationship between a customer and the supplier. A supplier must become a trusted companion. Customers will not only trust the company but they will also make their purchasing plans known at an early stage. In the consumer market, the trust that a brand enjoys is important. This guarantees certainty, as well as the connection with a target group. This leads to trust in the brand, similar to the trust in a company or person that can arise through personal contacts.
- The last basic principle formulated by Wiersema (1997) is the relationship with a market leader. This certainty and trust will also be reflected on the collaboration and in this case on the platform. Particularly if certain business functions are shared, such as the case with platforms, mutual dependency and interest will arise. This applies, for example, to the business functions such as marketing, finance and logistics. This is not only a typical feature of platforms in the so-called B2B market but also with Bol.com and Amazon. Independent businesses strove towards market leadership in the old economy, while new businesses find market leadership in the network, in the collaboration.

These days it is important that we also see this ambition with platforms. The old rules of market leadership still apply, only now they apply to a platform.

A Unique Value Compared with the Other Providers

For individual companies it is important that they have a strategy for creating value that is unique compared with the other providers within the network. This is in line with the previously mentioned vision of Treacy and Wiersema, as this value-creating strategy should also be difficult to copy for the competing companies, so that there is a long-lasting competitive advantage. A value proposition that is difficult to copy is one way to obtain a competitive advantage; the other way involves the advantage of the first mover. The first mover of a new concept has considerable value. This value lies in matters such as the creation of a network for the supply chain, the creation of regular clients and the acquisition of a good reputation and brand awareness. By optimising this head start and growing quickly, these newcomers can be disruptive to traditional providers and traditional market structures. In other words, the first innovator has many advantages, while those who do not respond quickly will have to work hard to catch up. This means that as soon as this first innovator has captured a market position, it will be in a strong position that is difficult to overtake by the current competition as well as other newcomers. Amazon, Thuisbezorgd.nl and Booking.com are good examples of this.

Who Will Become the New Competitors?

A shift has come about in the competition strategy as a result of the Internet, worldwide connectivity and new technologies. The five forces model that defines the competition strategy therefore has to be reassessed. Having control of unique resources or enjoying the benefits of one's large-scale infrastructure are no longer enough in holding back the competition. New technologies and the Internet enable competitors and start-ups to avoid traditional structures and barriers by using the value of information and interaction and by encouraging the co-creation of value (collaboration). In this way, companies create new markets instead of operating within the boundaries of the traditional markets. What is more, the exponential growth of tech companies compels businesses to concentrate on innovation and flexibility instead of fighting over the same metaphorical slice of cake, in a zero-sum game.

The exponential speed at which technology is developing has changed the way companies are structured. Nearly every company uses some form of technology for creating or delivering their products or services. The speed at which technology progresses forces companies to adapt to the ensuing changes. Companies with hierarchical structures are slow to adapt to changes, resulting in their lagging behind those competitors who are able to adapt. That is why it is important that companies are as structured as possible. It makes them more flexible and allows them to adapt quickly when necessary. That is why flexibility has become an important aspect of competitiveness.

One of the most important and valuable resources that a business can have is data. Every click that a customer makes on a website can be stored. A single click does not tell you very much, but when thousands or even millions of clicks are stored, then companies have access to valuable raw data. In order to utilise the value of this data, it has to be analysed with an algorithm or by running a mechanical process through the data set. The insights gained from this data analysis can be used to improve the services and to take better decisions based on customer behaviour. This increase of data also makes it easier to understand the customer. Analyses enable customers to be segmented into highly specific groups, making it much simpler to identify them and so save time and money on marketing. The manner in which a company selects and uses data has a major effect on its chances of success, and is therefore an important aspect of competition. The vision for the future describes data as providing the most important resource for competition. Without good data and without good analysis systems there is no future. Competition will be based on algorithms. It is as simple as that.

The future will be dominated by platforms and networks that form not only the basis of competition against traditional organisations but also against one another. Three types of competition arise as a result. These are as follows:

- First of all, the competition between producers. The producers still compete through products or services, but these are now offered on a platform based on the needs of individual customers.
- Second, competition between platforms. Platforms may face competition from new platforms or from traditional platforms that want to expand into a new market.
- Third, there is also competition between platforms and producers. Producers can create their own network within a platform and try to pull this network out of the platform. Platforms will have to avoid this.

Is Marketing Still a Competition Tool?

Marketing is important for the ecosystem of a platform. A platform uses marketing to attract visitors/buyers. The more visitors/buyers a platform attracts, the more producers will want to join the platform. The most valuable asset that a platform has is its users; the more users there are, the stronger the network effects. Platforms not only have to get users through strong marketing but those users already on the platform also have to be satisfied to such an extent that they want to remain loyal to the platform and provide positive word-of-mouth advertising. In order to achieve this, platforms have to optimise their functionality. The idea behind a platform is to connect producers and consumers in as frictionless way as possible. In order to facilitate this, an infrastructure has to be created that is both functional and easy to access. The functionality of a platform is determined by various functions, which are as follows:

- Firstly, the recommendation system is one of the most important functions of a platform. This ensures that every customer sees products that best suit his or her needs without having to look for them.
- Secondly, a platform's search function is very important. By having search functionality with the right filters, customers can find products quickly and easily.
- Furthermore, the visual display of the platform is important. In order to increase interactions and transactions on a platform, it is important that producers can display their products or content in an appealing manner. The visuals of a platform influence the visitors' behaviour. Consumers (visitors) are less likely to walk into an old, shabby shop, let alone buy products. The same applies to a visually unappealing platform.
- Other functions that add value to a platform are customer service, a range of secure payment methods and reviews. Customer satisfaction can increase through optimisation and adding functions. It is important that the value of the ecosystem is greater than the value of the functions of the platform; having superior functions does not offer any competitive advantages in themselves.

Another way for platforms to gain a competitive advantage is to use data. By analysing the data of the platforms, the functions can be optimised, such as filtering and matching, and gaining knowledge about the customers. Using this knowledge, derived from the data, platforms can constantly improve their ecosystem and make modifications according to customer needs. The data are analysed and translated further into algorithms. These algorithms analyse the search and buying behaviour, and look for indicators that say more about the person buying or searching. These algorithms therefore activate actions without the intervention of humans. Platforms that have mastered the use of data will have a competitive advantage over those platforms that struggle to do so. An example of this is Twitter. Compared with other social media companies such as Instagram and Facebook, Twitter knows very little about its users and therefore loses market share. Information is shared on Twitter, but there is usually no interaction or dialogue. As a result, any knowledge about the Twitter user is restricted to the particular focus area. Another advantage of data analysis is that it can detect the improper use of users. The platform would then be able to monitor the person (or bot) and stop the account if necessary, in order to protect the ecosystem of the platforms. The analyses and algorithms make it possible to guide future behaviour and allow better predictions to be made of future developments. We also see this in, for example, the medical world whereby algorithms can determine the indicators of certain illnesses and compare the results with healthy people. It can then be determined what the chance is that healthy people develop the same disease. These predictions are much more accurate than one would get from a doctor (Fry, 2018) (Figure 1).[3]

In the future, almost all producers will compete on platforms. This convergence, collaboration, means that independent companies will lose a great deal of their competitiveness. Whereas in the past producers had to focus on marketing in order to attract customers, producers on platforms only have to focus on keeping their consumers satisfied. The reason for this is that platforms do the marketing to attract customers to the platform themselves. In order to give themselves the chance to compete, the producers must comply with the rules imposed by these platforms. These rules can differ from sector to sector. Uber, for example, is

---

[3] Fry, Hannah (2018). *Hello World*, Transworld Publishers, Penguin Books, London, UK, p. 79 ff.

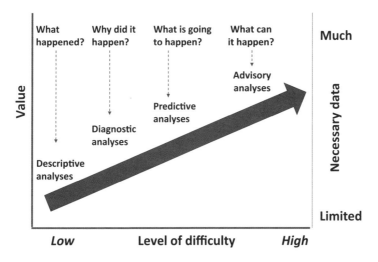

Figure 1.   Change in the focus of analyses.

Note: The use of data determines an organisation's success. The appropriate analyses, however, must be applied when doing so.

more regulated than YouTube. As a result of this, the producers are compelled to manoeuvre within these rules in their competition with one another. It is almost impossible for companies to compete without being part of a platform. The companies that form part of a platform benefit so much from the network effects that it will no longer be possible for those who are not part of a platform to survive alongside these platforms; let alone win the competition against the producers that are on the platform.

In recent years, there has been a shift in the way producers compete with one another. As described earlier, the interactions between them and the customers form the basis for a competitive advantage. This change will become even more important in the future. The producers can only gain a competitive advantage if they have many frequent customers. It is becoming more difficult for producers to win the loyalty of customers who are no longer loyal to one particular brand, but to a platform that offers practically every brand. Platforms have made it difficult for producers to win customer loyalty, so producers feel compelled to take advantage of the benefits these platforms offer (see the loyalty loop on page 69). Customers use filters to find the products that best suit their wishes. It is now essential that the producers on these platforms are able to match as many of these filters as possible. This is done by analysing popular searches and filters that are used by customers, and on that basis modify the products or the product description where necessary.

What Changes Will Take Place?

Market leadership arises as a consequence of a process of change, modifications and relevance for customers.

There has to be a shared ambition with clear aims. The battle for the customer is no longer a solo activity, but a shared network activity between all parties, compressed within a single platform.

Change 1: Competitive strengths are utilised in the platform/ network business model

Platform companies facilitate the interactions between producers and consumers, whereby much of the value is created by this network of external users of the platform. This shifts the strategy focus from internal optimisation to the maximisation of external interactions.

This makes the driving forces behind platform companies different. The exponential growth of the network-based platform strategy leads to monopolies based on the demand side of the economy, where supply and demand come together. A major weakness of Porter's five forces model is that it does not take account of the value created by network effects. Instead of preventing new or substitute products or services, it is the external forces in this strategy that actually add value to the platform. As a result, the power of suppliers and customers, which in traditional companies is regarded as a threat, is actually a competitive advantage in a platform company.

The operational boundaries become blurred, causing a shift from industrial rivalry to network rivalry. And thanks to the power of strong relationships within the network and an enormous customer base, it is also much easier to expand to new business sectors. An example of this is Google, which was set up as an online search engine but has since also become active in other areas such as home automation systems, mobile phone operating systems, voice recognition, cloud services and self-driving cars. As a result of these types of shifts, a platform can abruptly transform the traditional competition and structures within a sector. With its self-driving cars Google has become a direct competitor of General Motors. Companies that do not create a platform for themselves, or do not integrate their company within traditional platforms, will probably face more pressure on their margins if they compete against platform companies that can utilise various sources of income.

Change 2: From ownership to coordination of resources

The resource-based view of strategy focuses the management's attention on the company's internal resources in order to identify those assets, capacities and competences that have the potential to achieve competitive advantages. These are resources that the company owns and/or controls. In linear companies, these resources would involve both material assets such as factories, equipment and raw materials, as well as immaterial resources such as brands and intellectual property. In a platform business model, however, products and/or services are not produced by the platform itself. Production processes are not organised by the organisation either. As a result, there is no control over the creation of value within the production process. This value is brought in by external producers and is coordinated by the platform company. The owner of the platform creates value as an independent intermediary by matching and connecting these producers (supply), and facilitating direct interaction between consumers (demand). The network of external producers and consumers is a platform company's most important capital.

Change 3: From a focus on customer value to one on the value of ecosystems

Linear companies with classic strategic models aim to maximise the lifetime value of individual customers of products and/or services. These customers are located at the end of the linear process of B2C. Platforms, on the other hand, want to maximise the total value of a growing network, where the network consists of both users that supply products and/or services on the one hand and users that buy them on the other. These users can switch roles or even simultaneously have different roles. Users can, for example, take a ride in an Uber taxi today and be an Uber driver tomorrow; travellers can stay the night at an Airbnb and be an Airbnb host to travellers themselves another time. This change in the value chain is an important feature of a two-sided market.

Bibliography

Treacy, M. (1995). *The Discipline of Market Leaders: Choose Your Customers, Narrow Your Focus, Dominate Your Market,* contributed by Frederik Derk Wiersema, Addison-Wesley Publishing Company, p. 208.

Chapter 4

From Supply Chain to Network

The old distribution structure was based on a pipeline — linear, that is, a process from manufacturer, via various links such as wholesaler, distributors, dealers, agents and shops, to the customer. Each link had to contribute to the process and had their own value. This distribution model was a sales-oriented model in which the physical articles successively moved along to the next link in the chain. Very little information was shared, and usually it was only functional information regarding the product, sales price and complaints.

Customer data were not integrated, but was owned by each separate link in the chain. The organisations within this pipeline have an hierarchical structure with strict processes and clearly defined functions. This produces an efficient organisation with low costs and strong internally focused control. The connections are commercial and part of the total pipeline. The success depends on the total process (chain) all the way down to the end user. With the arrival of the Internet, webshops emerged which simply copied this pipeline without really taking advantage of the new possibilities.

With a platform, the connection between the parties is based on network connections. The platform is an intermediary between production (an hierarchical organisation) and the market (dynamic). A platform is often used to compensate for the limitations of the hierarchical organisation. This applies to business functions that require greater flexibility, such as purchasing, research, information technology (IT) and sales. The platforms fulfil a specific mediating function, involving independent parties (as participants). This can eventually lead to an organisation that is completely based on collaboration with other parties as well as collaboration in one or more platforms.

A company as a separate organisation and independent entity will disappear; the competitive strength will be entirely determined by the platform. In a pipeline approach, competition was based on the end product with all the relevant elements: from design to price and efficient distribution. Within the pipeline each link would compete against similar companies, resulting in individual competition per link. The competition is based on the distribution process (the chain) and the products offered. With networks and platforms, this linear supply chain with sub-optimisations is replaced by a supply ecosystem, involving an optimisation of information, knowledge and collaboration, from producer to buyer.

As mentioned previously, the externally oriented functions lend themselves best to collaboration within a platform; such as sales, purchasing and research. The strength of the platform lies in the sharing of knowledge, costs and resources (technology). There are three types of platforms that have sales as an objective, which are as follows:

- A collective webshop consisting of suppliers, sometimes with a link to the companies' own webshops. Sometimes by showing the collaborating parties (with a link) according to subject. This is an affiliate platform.
- An aggregator. An aggregator is a host that offers other providers facilities that allow them to also offer their products and services. Here, use can be made of the attractiveness of the host and the available facilities.
- And finally, a multisided platform (MSP) that, as an independent party, matches the individual demand with an individual supply (product based).

An aggregator can be described as a business model for electronic trade whereby a company collects information on its website about goods and/or services from various competing sources, or offers products from various competing providers (for example, Bol.com in the Netherlands).

An aggregator is a sales model, also referred to as a single-sided platform, which has a strong focus on sales. Central to an MSP, however, is the matching of needs (based on an individual demand).

MSPs are technologies, products or services that create value, primarily by enabling direct interactions between two or more customer or participants groups such as providers and consumers (for example, Booking.com or Airbnb.com).

An MSP is a customer-oriented platform, on which competition takes place through the matching of needs. Satisfying the buyer's needs is more important than the product elements. This makes a platform not only disruptive in markets but also always a winner in the competition against the pipeline, with as end station a dealer, distributor or shop. The platform leads to lower costs, greater impact on the market, customer loyalty and an individual offer based on the matching of these needs.

Traditional organisations are slow to adopt the new technologies that form the foundation of these new platforms. These traditional organisations are consequently quickly attacked by the newcomers that conquer the market with their superior power and often large amounts of money. The collaboration within the platform leads to greater clout and impact, with the network being the facilitative factor. As suppliers are connected to customers through an algorithm of matching and connectivity at product need level, the platform takes over the function of the distribution channel. It can deliver the product directly; a distributor or shop, however, can also play a role in this provided it adds value such as stocks, advice, speedy delivery and extra services. If there is no added value, the role of all intermediaries will disappear or be minimised.

It is not only technology-driven platforms that are becoming more dominant but physical platforms such as shopping centres also fulfil a platform role: by bringing together supply and demand, attracting buyers and attracting shops. The essence of this is to make this physical platform attractive for visitors, and therefore also for providers.

These physical platforms' are so appealing that they attract many visitors, and so are interesting for providers. It is because these centres are so attractive to buyers that old centres, such as local shopping centres or city centres, have to compete in winning the interest of visitors. The current developments show that this has not always been successful by a long way.

This change in the buying behaviour of consumers ultimately has a strong influence on retailers' establishment strategy, and can be seen by the establishment policy of new retailers setting themselves up in the Netherlands. These retailers often opt for just a select number of cities that have a strong appeal. This select approach to choosing a location to establish a business is in part due to the omni-channel way of thinking; a significant proportion of consumers can be served from the webshop and receive support from a physical shop at a (limited) distance. This all leads to some municipalities having too many empty shops, which are not necessarily replaced by new formulas.

The outflow impact to other cities and online channels is so much greater than the turnover growth that can be realised from the population growth that the traditional numbers of shops can be considered too large now as well as for the future.

This will certainly be the case if the objective of many retailers to generate 20% of their turnover through online sales is realised. For this reason, the focus of many municipalities will have to shift from measures that stimulate demand to supply-driven measures that lead to the appropriate number of shops for the shop space required by the retailers (Dynamis, 2017).[1]

Business-to-Business

In the area of purchasing there is a collaboration between providers, usually intended for industrial companies or so-called business-to-business (B2B) companies. Examples of this are auctions, tendering platforms, resource platforms and capacity platforms. Other examples

---

[1] https://dynamis.nl/uploads/media/25/global/Sprekende%20Cijfers%20Winkelmarkten/Sprekende%20Cijfers%20Winkelmarkten%202017%20sept.pdf.

include DH Gate, Global Source and Trade Key. There are also platforms for purchasing resources, raw materials, electricity, used machines and transport.

These platforms make the offer transparent and increase the reach for providers. This places the role of the wholesaler increasingly under pressure. The old traditional role of the wholesaler was to collect and store products which were then distributed further to the next link in the supply chain, who are often dealers, distributors or retailers. The changes as already described will lead to new connections being created in the platform or a network. The direct relationships that result from this will actually make wholesalers redundant, unless they reassess their role. The basic function of a wholesaler can remain, provided there is some need for a collection or distribution function. A wholesaler would then put the products into groups to then sell them on to, for example, shops or factories. The advantage here is that the buying party would not have to personally approach the various suppliers individually to obtain the products or parts. A direct connection is possible if this is a link between a supplier and the customer. The suppliers must be able to meet a customer's requirements in terms of speed, availability and delivery. If they are not able to do this effectively, then this is a function for the wholesaler or distributor (or the network).

A second function of a wholesaler is the collecting function. With deliveries by numerous suppliers, which have to be combined to a single delivery to the customer, and perhaps accompanied by a single invoice, the wholesaler can fulfil this aggregation function and arrange the storage and shipping.

A third function is the post-processing function. We see direct deliveries particularly from manufacturers of ready-to-use products that do not require any further processing. Some products, however, do need some further work before being shipped on. An adjustment to the size, printing, additional products or perhaps installation. A wholesaler/distributor can carry out this work prior to the final delivery. It is clear that a network approach and platforms pose a threat to wholesalers/distributors in their traditional activities. There therefore has to be a reassessment of their basic functions: collection, distribution supplemented with transition activities (modifications). If wholesalers are able to adapt their activities to the wishes of the customer and the possibilities of the suppliers, they may still be able to offer something of benefit.

Also, at a research level, we see increasingly more collaboration in a platform structure where knowledge, experience and best practices are shared in order to help one another to compete more effectively and thereby become more successful. Increasingly often, companies share information as this helps to promote cost reductions on the one hand and to create added value through carrying out joint research on the other.

More and more platforms are created based on expertise or problematic issues. A simple example are the Internet fora or communities that deal with particular problem areas with specialists answering questions. These can be amateur specialists, as seen with various technical issues, where users try to help one another out. But there are also professional specialists. In the healthcare sector it is possible to participate in a knowledge database, but this, too, is linked to specific support. A highly specific application is the sharing of knowledge through a knowledge platform. This type of platform shares blogs and videos from experts on a particular subject. Many universities use these knowledge platforms to share lectures online, give webinars or make an entire course, or even degree study, available online through videos (Stanford is an example of this with coursera.com).

Confidentiality is, of course, very important when sharing information. Particularly with these research platforms a login procedure, and often ballotage, is required. This is less important when sharing study material as one is simply consuming knowledge without participating in it. Login details, however, are usually still asked in order to get a better picture of the users and their needs. Uploading one's own blogs or papers is also encouraged.

How are Networks Applied?

The use of networks and network-based collaborations began at the start of this century. As previously described, this occurred under pressure from greatly changing market conditions. Due to the use and the growing popularity of the Internet, there was also an increase in competition, along with increasing pressure on the prices and margins among traditional providers. Organisations tried to improve their efficiency by, for example, abandoning unprofitable activities and outsourcing cost centres to specialised companies. This led to, for example, car leasing, debt factoring, renting premises and even to an increased use of temporary staff (through companies such as Taskrabbit.com). Other resources were shared such as computer facilities and software, and cloud applications, whereby products were offered as a service.

In order to manage this change, good collaboration between all parties was required. This need for efficiency and specialisation was reinforced by the development of the technology. Technology made it possible to coordinate (orchestrate) and monitor all functions and activities. Later the technology also enabled resources to be made more flexible through cloud applications, thereby changing the *ownership* of resources into the *use* of resources (sharing), with the company's own IT facilities changing into the use of IT facilities. Licence contracts were no longer required, but rather subscription contracts. Ownership was no longer important, but use.

The Internet is reforming the manner in which companies create value. This is causing considerable ripple effects in all industries and creating an entirely new business sector. These changes are being driven by the following three different factors:

- improvements in the collaboration (through networks);
- decentralised production;
- the rise of artificial intelligence.

Platforms ensure that everyone within that platform not only works together but also complements or exchanges value with one another. Each consumer can become a producer or provider and adds value to the platform. Roles can change, but so too can the buying process (based on needs and association). What is more, the platform becomes a dominant party in the market, and causes the old independent parties with an outdated business model to shrink and lose their competitive strength. This is an important transition from the business model of suppliers to that of consumers, i.e., an MSP.

An MSP does, however, require close collaboration between providers. The collaboration must be on the basis of adding value (including the decentralised production) and new technologies are used as innovation for all those involved.

These MSPs now have the following two specific roles:

(1) To provide an accessible infrastructure where both consumers and providers (producers) can participate and exchange information with one another as well as communicate.
(2) To help anyone who participates in this exchange and to mediate in this value exchange: information, sales and other transactions.

As we have seen, the old model of a supply chain was linear. The new model is a constant feedback model between consumers and providers (producers), whereby the value is created not by the producer but by the interaction. This model is based on an interactive network model (Figure 1).

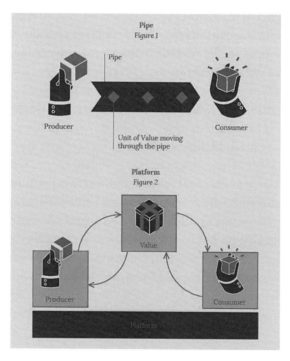

Figure 1.   Structure of platforms with supply and demand (Choudary, 2015, p. 26).

The Transformation from a Supply Chain to a Platform[2]

(1) *The shift in markets: From consumers as the endpoint to producers as the endpoint*

Before platforms, the consumer was located at the receiving end of the pipeline. The demand was therefore matched by the product supply, and the consumer had to choose from a range of products. The consumer paid with money and loyalty. The competition was between the various providers at product level. Since the emergence of MSPs, the consumer is no longer the receiving party but a partner in the demand–supply match. The consumer can now also be a provider (of products or services) such as with Airbnb and Uber. That is why the platforms need to shift their attention from following consumers to attracting products and consumers as well as ensuring there is a good match. This is actually also the function of the shop. However, shops have not been able to compete due to the expertise inequality (customers often know more than the shop simply by "googling"), the lack of personnel able to provide advice and the limited range of products that result in an ineffective facilitative function.

(2) *The shift in competitive advantage: From resources (products) to ecosystems (network)*

Before platforms, competition was based on the competitive advantage gained from resources and intellect. This American (Anglo-Saxon) form of competition, the bigger the better, is no longer relevant. The platform now determines the competitive value of products and the appeal to consumers. The basis for this is the ecosystem (network) that ensures a connection. The large platforms have a strong appeal to providers and consumers, as can be seen with Alibaba, Airbnb and Uber. It is not only all about the match between needs and supply, and the link with supplementary products and services but also the orchestration between physical and digital resources such as holiday homes and taxis.

We see a strong leverage here, which creates enormous value. It is not the access to physical resources that creates value, but the leverage; the

---

[2] Choudary, Sangreet Paul, *The Platform Scale*, pp. 27–29.

network effects (such as exponential growth without extra costs). The network effect between the range of products and services provided and the need. For example, internationalisation, whereby a platform using the Internet can also be very active in other markets. Adding other providers or products is easy and costless, and immediately leads to extra revenue (zero cost expansion).

A wide range of associated products can also be offered, as is seen in the rapidly growing number of platforms. If there is sufficient knowledge of the buyers, the needs and buying motives, what is on offer does not need to be restricted to just one product or service. This will help to increase the turnover of a platform exponentially. The relevance for visitors and buyers will also increase. Holiday providers offer not only places to stay but they also arrange air travel, taxis, car rental, restaurant reservations and sometimes clothing. This results in a strong focus on the share of wallet.

(3) *The shift in value creation: From processes to interactions*

Before the introduction of platforms there was an *end-to-end* process, which formed the value creation, from product to user (supply chain effect). Since the emergence of MSPs, the value creation has been determined by interaction between producers and users. Value is no longer made and increased through processes, which organise internal activities and resources (as Porter had clearly described based on the classic business model). Instead, value is created and increased through interactions that provide the orchestration between consumers and the supply in the new ecosystem (network).

First Phase of Applications

The first phase during which networks, based on the Internet, were used was based on the modification of old patterns and processes. The technology was used in order to facilitate and optimise the process. Decisions at that time were made on the basis of returns, not on impact. This partly explains why traditional organisations were slow to adopt new technologies. Decisions were taken based on return on investment (ROI), not on the basis of competitive strength and customers' wishes. The market and the preferences of customers did change, however. Due to the strong internal orientation of decision-makers and the focus on efficiency, there was no good contact with the market (customers). Competition was based on old instruments such as price, product, place and promotion. Traditional providers were taken by surprise by the new start-ups, which were not only based on the latest technologies but also had an aggressive growth model. A defensive strategy was often the response to this development; as we have seen with shops, in the retail sector, hotels and, of course, taxi companies (based on platforms). This defensive strategy is actually also used by other providers as an answer to changes in the market. We saw this (and still do) with physical shops when they responded to the cheaper products offered by Alibaba and Amazon. Traditional organisations are too much inclined to be led by their traditional position and processes, whereby they did not (and some still do not) take the new developments into account. As a result, they responded too late to the new entrants. Nokia and its mobile telephones are a classic example of this. They had no answer at all to the arrival of the iPhone (in 2007), but continued focusing on trying to make their telephone even better while the preference of customers quickly shifted towards a telephone with Internet applications and instant messaging (such as WhatsApp). The Nokia management appeared paralysed and continued to insist that everything would turn out fine, even after the takeover by Microsoft. A defensive response based on the traditional supply is commonly seen. Another response is the confusion or panic that can arise as a result of coming against new start-ups. Management boards often trivialise the developments (as did Nokia) or respond in an exaggerated and uncoordinated manner. There is often a lack of strategy or knowledge of the changes.

We saw this happen in the hotel sector, which did not respond adequately to Booking.com and then later Airbnb. Hotels no longer seemed to understand their customers, and their customers' choices, while they were in a strong position with the information they had on their customers as well as the possibility of putting their reservation systems online. The response of restaurants to Takeaway and Deliveroo is very similar. The response to Uber was also one of dismissiveness and underestimating the threat. The Uber system essentially does not differ from the traditional taxi system, except that Uber's is based on transparency and customer wishes, and is facilitated by the traditional Internet technology (an app).

'The Internet? We are not interested in it.'
                                              — *Bill Gates, 1993*

'I see little commercial potential for the Internet for at least 10 years.'
                                              — *Bill Gates, 1994*[3]

Steve Ballmer, the former CEO of Microsoft, 10 years later made a similar mistake as Bill Gates, after the introduction of the iPhone. Completely denying the potential and acceptance by customers, Microsoft obstinately clung on to the idea that the mobile phone was solely a means of communication for text and voice. The subsequent success of the iPhone showed that Microsoft's 'defensive' response was an expensive error. Its takeover of Nokia's mobile telephone division was a flop and the later Microsoft variations of the mobile phone did not offer any distinctive features of its own compared with the iPhone. After this, Microsoft decided to shift its focus to infrastructural applications, an area in which they were already successful with the desktop computer. For traditional cloud applications they are among the market leaders (Azure, along with Amazon cloud in particular), as well as in software developments for platforms (outsystems, dotnet and Azure).

> 'There's no chance that the iPhone is going to get any significant market share. No chance,' said Ballmer. 'It's a $500 subsidized item. They may make a lot of money. But if you actually take a look at the 1.3 billion phones that get sold, I'd prefer to have our software in 60% or 70% or 80% of them, than I would to have 2% or 3%, which is what Apple might get.'
>
> It's [the Zune phone] not a concept you'll ever get from us. We're in the Windows Mobile business. We wouldn't define our phone experience just by music. A phone is really a general purpose device. You want to make telephone calls, you want to get and receive messages, text, e-mail, whatever your preference is. The phone really is kind of a general purpose device that we need to have clean and easy to use.[4]

---

[3] *Source*: https://gcn.com/articles/2010/11/26/33-classic-it-quotes.aspx.

[4] *Source*: https://arstechnica.com/information-technology/2007/04/ballmer-says-iphone-has-no-chance-to-gain-significant-market-share/.

The Second Phase of Applications

A platform comprises a total supply, the products database and the inter-action between historical buying behaviour, the knowledge of the analyses and the interaction with suppliers and like-minded people (the commu-nity feel). It is this interaction that forms the basis of a platform, with a demand-driven supply based on needs instead of a supply-driven one. The focus clearly lies on the value creation for an increasing number of provid-ers and a growing number of consumers. The value will grow exponen-tially as increasingly more providers participate, attracting increasingly more consumers. This creates a dominant position in the market, also referred to as the network effect. The increase in products and services results in more consumers. This larger supply allows for more efficient matching. A wide range of products creates added value for visitors; after all, on this platform they can find whatever they want. This is how Amazon, Alibaba, Airbnb and others are able to attract growing numbers of potential visitors, making these platforms even more interesting for evermore providers. This network effect determines the popularity and size of the platform, but is also a decisive factor for the market value. The necessity to join a platform grows ever stronger as a result. The competi-tive value of a provider decreases as a platform becomes more successful in the market. The only option that is left then is to become a niche player, offering specialist products and services to a specific target group. These niche players can, however, cause the large platforms trouble, providing that they really do provide something distinctive in their product or ser-vices. Alongside a platform there is only room left for niche players.

Which Network Effects are Disruptive?

The network effect can be clearly seen in the relationship between costs and revenue. Its effect and that of virtual products (referred to as *zero-costing* products) lead to a rapidly growing turnover and moderately grow-ing costs. The profit contribution increases exponentially as a result, which can be seen in Figure 2. For physical products there will be a more or less fixed relationship between the costs and revenue. For platforms the reve-nue will not be related to the costs. The technology ensures for a moderate growth in the costs and an exponential growth in turnover.

By the Numbers: Amazon

CATEGORY	1996	1999
Employees	151	7,600
Revenue (US$)	$5.1M	$1.64B
Customer accounts	180K	16.9M

Figure 2.   Relationship between revenue and costs for Amazon.com.

This effect can also be seen with other platform and network-based providers. An example is Google's search engine. There is no relationship here between searching and costs. There is a relationship, however, between the number of providers and the advertising costs. The more 'searchers' there are, the more interesting Google is for advertisers, particularly when linked to a search. Popular searches also mean that the amount a company is willing to pay for an advertisement (for example, via AdWords) increases. In addition, the general advertising revenue will also increase. The effects of this (network) effect can be seen in Figure 3.

Examination of this data clearly shows that the focus of network-based companies is aimed at attracting visitors, and thereby suppliers. The disappearance of the close relationship between costs and revenue leads to lower costs and consequently higher profitability.

By the Numbers: Google

CATEGORY	2001	2007
Employees	284	16,805
Revenue (US$)	$86M	$16.6B
Searches per year	27B	372B

CHANGE OVER TIME

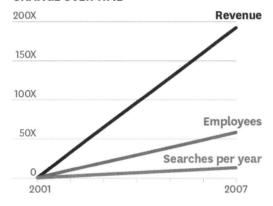

Figure 3.   Relationship between turnover and costs for Google.

Another network effect is the two-sided market: a market for providers and consumers. The platform mediates between both parties, and is in effect 'the market'. Competition used to take place in the market with a limited number of providers and a limited number of consumers. The platform attracts both providers and visitors that make use of the platform (the independent party). The platform stimulates a market whereby providers compete against one another based on the consumers' needs. This helps to create more knowledge of the buying process, while at the same time it becomes easier for consumers to compare the products and services on offer. As the focus lies on matching demand with the supply using filters, it is no longer a matter of selling products but rather matching the supply with the needs of the buyer. This value exchange forms the basis of the interaction and appeal. The better a platform does this, the more consumers it will attract, thereby also making the platform increasingly interesting for providers.

These two network effects lead to a different sort of competition, but also to the great value that is attached to such platforms as Airbnb and Uber.

Will the Visitors of Platforms Become More Powerful?

Platforms and network effects are competition factors that Porter could not have foreseen back in the 1980s. The five-forces model was based on external factors that had an influence on the market and 'attacked' the turnover of traditional parties. As a result, barriers had to be built in order to protect a company's position. With a platform strategy, both buyers and sellers have a mutual interest. A strong focus on attracting individual visitors is part of the demand economy. This makes it more difficult to attack these platforms as an ecosystem. The traditional knowledge of the behaviour of customers and the response to suppliers is a barrier in itself. We see this with Facebook, for example, which has so much information about its users that this immediately makes it a bonding factor. Leaving Facebook is actually not an option, as you would lose all your contacts as well as everything that connects you with the platform (suggestions) and your friends. Platforms nonetheless have to remain alert for any changes. This could be new entrants (such as Instagram), shifts in the wishes of customers (FaceTime as an alternative to Skype) or legislation that may negatively affect the revenue model (such as privacy legislation). Competition may arise slowly, but it can still pose a threat. When WhatsApp was small, it was in its own way a threat for Facebook, as was Instagram, until they were bought by Facebook. Both new entrants had a different communication model with customers. As this communication medium became popular it could have become a threat to Facebook, which is also communication based. A same-sided platform (people with people).

There are various types of platforms that have arisen through users having a particular bond with them. This could be vloggers (KOL, *key opinion leaders* in China) that have managed to win over the loyalty of many fans, or perhaps even Google, which as a search engine can offer more and more social media aspects (an example is Google Shopping, based on Google Search or Google Maps). The role of vloggers and Instagram can also be considerable among certain buyers groups.

A niche player could arrive on the market with a sophisticated offer that differs from the traditional providers, as previously mentioned. An example of the 'old' economics being confronted with applications based on technology. Data can also form the basis for a new concept. Knowledge databases can make customers more assertive, forcing traditional providers to change. Examples of this can be found in the healthcare sector, where the many knowledge systems provide visitors with comprehensive information about ailments, analyses and treatments. This erodes the role of the family doctor somewhat, who often also ends up getting into discussions with a better informed and opinionated patient. A seven-minute appointment at a doctor's surgery is then too short. This puts more pressure on the GP and leads to unsatisfied patients whose trust and confidence in the doctor is damaged in part due to a short and overly functional consultation.

The impact on traditional markets depends on the innovative character of a platform and the acceptance by the market parties. For a niche provider, the impact on the total market will not be that great, but in the specific market segment it can, of course, have a significant effect. A niche player is never dominant in the total market, but can still be troublesome for larger parties. The large platforms, the dominant players, will not only have to give up some of the market share to niche players but will also feel the effects of specialist platforms in the areas of knowledge, information and research. It is the transparency of these platforms and the educational character that lead to a better or more well-founded purchasing decision. The level of knowledge of the customer exceeds the information provided by the dominant platforms (which are usually sales-oriented). The MSPs are dominant in markets and are disruptive. They connect the supply with demand, and *vice versa*, thereby creating their own sort of market with competition between the providers. There is an interaction between a platform's providers and visitors. The number of visitors and their return behaviour determine to a large degree whether the platform is of interest to providers. We also saw this with magazines; the more subscribers they had, the more attractive they were to advertisers. When the number of subscribers fell, advertisers increasingly lost interest. The revenue model,

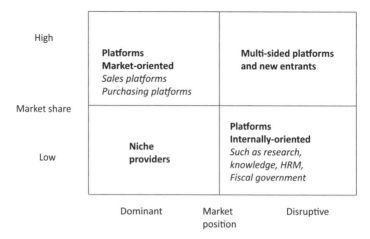

Figure 4.   Market position of platforms.

with advertising as well as sales revenues, came under pressure as a result. The power of buyers and visitors should therefore not be underestimated (Figure 4).

Other Applications of Networks: Binding Visitors, Customers and Suppliers

Another major difference between a supply chain-based distribution model and a platform is the control model. In a supply chain, distribution and sales are important business functions. The board of directors are accountable for the sales and profits (certainly in Anglo-Saxon companies). Every customer journey is regarded as a project, with the sale (transaction) as the end goal. In a platform, the number of visitors, the return behaviour and the share of wallet (the percentage of a customer's expenditure) are important control variables. There is no customer journey but a customer loop based on needs: matching and suggestions. The customers must return (as a result of satisfaction and communication) as the value of the platform is based on future turnover and profits (Figure 5).

The power of a platform lies in bonding visitors/customers, the growing number of interactions and the return business ratio. This is an

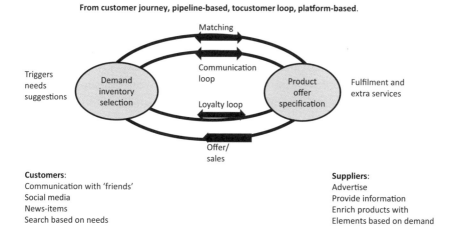

From customer journey, pipeline-based, tocustomer loop, platform-based.

Matching

Communication loop

Triggers
needs
suggestions

Demand
inventory
selection

Product
offer
specification

Fulfilment and
extra services

Loyalty loop

Offer/
sales

Customers:
Communication with 'friends'
Social media
News-items
Search based on needs

Suppliers:
Advertise
Provide information
Enrich products with
Elements based on demand

Figure 5. The customer loop.

Source: This diagram is partly based on the video clip: www.youtube.com/watch?v=EfRrD3we0Hg.

important part of the competitive advantage compared with supply chain businesses. Platforms are all to do with engaging customers and suppliers. Classic businesses, however, are more concerned with market share and transactions (turnover). The dominant platforms have managed to bond the market leaders to them, but they also have the most visitors, and consequently a greater impact on traditional markets. This explains why market leaders (platforms) have a large portion of the market share (on average 70%). An additional network effect, based on this bonding of customers, is the name recognition. Customer loyalty is won through increasingly more interactions, which is difficult to realise with a limited range of products. Successful platforms will expand their product portfolio and search for other promising markets. We can see this with Uber ('Uber eats', transport), Facebook and also Amazon and Bol.com. Customer loyalty and interaction are the key drivers here. The amount of time a visitor stays on a platform is increased through interaction. This can be achieved through reviews, social media activities (customers responding to other customers) and the integration of videos from the suppliers. Suppliers will want, after all, to inform visitors about their products, while customers may want to share their experiences with others. The platform, in turn, will want to facilitate this interaction based on needs and solutions. This leads to knowledge of the customers, which can then again form the basis for expanding the product portfolio as well as for the indicators of the algorithms driven by behavioural characteristics.

In short, as a result of digitalisation customers quickly experience a commodification[5] of their life in which the line between consumption and entertainment becomes blurred. The price that is paid is no longer based solely on the production and supply of a physical product; services and imaginary values now also play a role in the pricing. Technology has completely changed the customer journey, and is transforming it into a customer loop as described above. Thanks to big data and algorithms, businesses can now monitor customer behaviour more easily than ever before. Algorithms and data collection enable companies to provide their customers with a compelling and customisable experience. Burberry in London, for example, seamlessly connects the shop with an online experience. Large screens and RFID chips in the clothing give the shoppers information about how the item was produced and recommendations on how it can be worn. Marketing strategies are becoming increasingly more efficient and specific for the individual customer, saving time and money when it comes to investigating their needs. Companies are now able to predict the needs of consumers and respond to them, as well as involve them in producing content.

Do Networks and Platforms Change the Way Marketing is Used?

The evolution of the Internet forms the basis to a fundamental change in how consumers perceive brands and buy goods. The combination of media mobility and online content means that consumers now experience the greater part of their content and advertisements while being mobile, during which they are multitasking and active on several screens at the same time. Consumers are now actively looking for value in inexpensive purchases, and brands are becoming commoditised, which ultimately

---

[5]Commodification is the process whereby increasingly more aspects of human activities and their results are assigned a monetary value instead of the intrinsic or inherent value. The term was introduced by Karl Marx.

forms a bigger challenge for the modern marketing professional. The power of words no longer lies in the medium, but in the manner in which they are used in the medium. In particular, most organisations have started rebranding and changing the way they do business, using their resources to build interactive relationships with consumers in online communities. They try to create a network instead of pushing through media campaigns. A company's speed at which it can adapt and its versatility are crucial. If they are not quick enough, there will surely be a competitor who is.

A large proportion of customer behaviour is also influenced by *reviews*. Building a good customer relationship never stops when the deal for that excellent product has been closed; there always has to be excellent aftersales service. The Internet has made this even more essential than before. Nowadays consumers have access to word-of-mouth advertising and reviews, and can easily write electronic reviews themselves. Statistics show that 90% of consumers first read online reviews before visiting a company. And 88% of consumers trust these online reviews as much as they do personal recommendations. Satisfied customers, users and consumers write good reviews. The reviews of satisfied consumers cannot be bought by providers. It can be quite a challenge to get these reviews, as not everyone wants to share their experience, after visiting, for example, a restaurant. What is more, consumers prefer to trust the advice of other users or a familiar site that they trust. Consumers mistrust product marketing professionals, and so the brand supremacy and brand loyalty degenerate. That is why it is important for companies to find inventive ways of getting satisfied customers to leave a review. This can also be a perfect opportunity to get honest feedback and find out where things can be improved.

The pressure to be flexible as well as to respond to a change in customer expectations is considerable. It is clear that a platform needs a different control model, marketing and organisation than traditional businesses. This requires a different type of leadership (based more on customer information and indicators) and other key performance indicators (KPIs) than you see in classic organisations. Platforms will usually begin as start-ups, whereby the culture, leadership and market approach lie embedded within the DNA of the business. The entire business is marketing driven. The response to competition will also be fundamentally different from the feeling of being under threat by competition that so typifies traditional organisations (Alstyne, 2016).[6]

Another possible application of networks, which would cause businesses based on a supply chain to fall behind, is the *Internet of things.* This can take the connection of products, locations, movements and, of course, people to a whole new level. A smartphone allows all movements to be followed. All these products are connected to a network and provide a huge amount of data for the platform. This can lead to new applications based on data analyses. Through a smartphone, a platform can form the basis for communication at any desired location. New services can also be offered. *Location-based services* are an example of this. Google is busy developing such a network for a *smart home* using its *nest* concept. Connecting, for example, the doorbell, cameras, thermostat and smoke detectors, can provide information about the home and the energy use. This would then enable the energy consumption to be optimally adjusted to the owners' lifestyle. What is more, it would be possible to draw up specific energy contracts, offer security services and develop other services. In this example independent service providers are connected to the *nest platform.* This sort of concept would not be possible with a pipeline organisation. Amazon is developing a similar network around its Alexa concept, while Apple is developing its own *smart home* concept.

Platforms are becoming increasingly stronger through the focus on customer needs and long-term customer relationships, the digitalisation of products (no physical components) and the development of the network structure. Processes are modified based on the individual wishes, customisation and flexibility. A new business concept based on this digitalisation of processes, efficient matching of demand and supply and the optimisation of resources, is the basis of a platform. A platform is directed on the basis of value creation. At the heart of this is the share of the expenditure on a particular product (share of wallet). With further growth, the focus will remain on the share of wallet, but will increasingly

---

[6] An extensive analysis in Alstyne, Marchal W. Van *et al.* (2016). Pipelines, Platforms and the New Rules of Strategy, *Harvard Business Review.*

shift to a total share of wallet. This can be seen in, for example, the expansion of the products and services offered by Bol.com, Amazon.com and Coolblue.nl. The new concepts make use of the latest technological possibilities. That is why it is so difficult for traditional parties to compete. Traditional (pipeline) businesses are stuck to their old structures, old decision-making processes and old (transaction-oriented) control models with a limited range of products.

The Cloud as a Basis for a Network

A cloud can be used for all sorts of applications, such as sharing information, a system or a platform. The differences are shown in Figures 6(a) and 6(b).

In some apps a link is made with a physical location (such as a shopping area) and the shop and visitor. An integral network based on cloud applications forms the basis of these providers. With Uber, for example, a location-based connection is made between the taxi driver and the customer. Airbnb also provides support in the same way for the hosts of temporary lodgings. Cloud services (IaaS) are used to realise this. Cloud services are global networks and are accessible regardless of location. Data, systems and applications are all accessible via the cloud. Providers of services offer facilities such as these connections, as well as systems and applications as a service. These are often based on subscriptions or use. A Saas (systems as a service) model is an example of this, whereby the access to systems and the sharing of applications is offered as a service. The Paas (Platform as a Service) and iPaaS also operate in the same way. iPaaS is a platform for developing and implementing integrations in the cloud and between the cloud and the company. iPaaS users can develop integration flows, which connect applications in the cloud or at a particular location. No further hardware or middleware is required for this. This is the network that a platform uses.

> Providing further definition and specificity to the iPaaS category, Gartner outlines a number of key functions in its reference model. These include tools and technologies that support the execution of integration flows, the development and lifecycle management of integrations, the

Summary of Key Differences

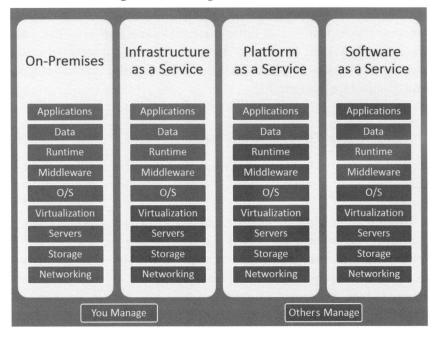

Figure 6(a).   The different applications of the Cloud. www.bmc.com.

SaaS	Google Apps, Dropbox, Salesforce, Cisco WebEx, Concur, GoToMeeting
PaaS	AWS Elastic Beanstalk, Windows Azure, Heroku, Force.com, Google App Engine, Apache Stratos, OpenShift
IaaS	DigitalOcean, Linode, Rackspace, Amazon Web Services (AWS), Cisco Metapod, Microsoft Azure, Google Compute Engine (GCE)

Figure 6(b).   The different applications of the Cloud.

management and monitoring of application flows, governance, and essential cloud features such as multitenancy, elasticity and self-provisioning. Gartner also sees iPaaS as a potential platform for the buying, selling, and exchange of integration flows (both out-of-the-box and custom-built patterns) between users, service providers, and integration providers.[7]

What Form of Organisation Best Suits a Network Structure or Platform?

Traditional organisations are usually based on the function the organisation fulfils in the supply chain. The organisation of these links is often hierarchical with a central point of control, the 'factory' and a supporting administrative department. Marketing is limited to advertising and participation on trade fairs. The final link is more customer-oriented, but with a focus on transactions and margins. Despite customers being essential for the continued existence of the organisation, marketing as a staff function is sometimes an operational function. Marketing is, however, seldom a strategic business function.

Hierarchical organisations have operational independence, which is (partly) lost when entering into partnerships. These partnerships can not only take the form of loose collaborations, such as with outsourcing but can also be very close ones such as with network partnerships. An organisation, with a close collaboration, can have a strong focus on its own strengths and its role within a network. If an activity can be carried out by another provider, then a structural connection is important. This collaboration not only offers opportunities but also threats because of the dependency on the network. This network must be an independent entity, with its own control and accountability.

There is therefore no longer a value chain with value activities that take place in linear sequence. And the consumer is no longer at the end of these processes but rather forms part of the value creation within a value network.

---

[7] *Source*: www.mulesoft.com/resources/cloudhub/what-is-ipaas-gartner-provides-reference-model.

This input can be used to put together a value network (Figure 7). This shows that the internal configuration of the platform company is different from that of traditional companies.

The organisation of the future must be part of a network with its own distinctive competence. It needs to be possible to connect the systems using APIs. In addition to the supply of products and services, the social function and hybrid support (website, mobile, sensors, IoT and AI) are also important.

Organisations that form part of a platform or a network, have to be able to respond quickly to questions, desires, behaviour and changes. What is more, the analyses of this behaviour provide a great deal of insights into customers' buying processes and buying motives. It makes

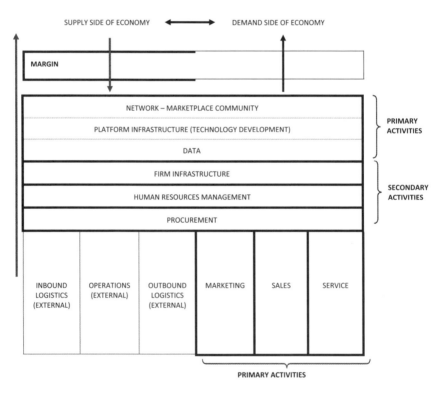

Figure 7.   Internal structure of a network organisation.

sense that an organisation needs to respond to this. Quick adaptations (agility), direct response (flexibility) and strategic adaptations are essential for success. In the network it is important to focus on one's own function in relation to the added value that the organisation can offer. This is a strategic principle. The HRM department also has to take into account this necessity to change quickly. The following clear choices constantly have to be made:

- whether job positions have to be on a permanent or a temporary basis;
- whether the job function fit the organisation or whether it is best to outsource/insource them;
- whether to take on permanent staff (which leads to less flexibility) or temporary staff, such as those on temporary contracts, or freelancers, or temporary staff through employment agencies, for greater flexibility.

> Approximately a quarter of the world's working population work flexible hours. Much of this growth is due to the increasing number of free-lancers. This flexibilisation will continue, regardless of what trade unions think of it. Trade unions want to see permanent contracts, but these go against the grain. In order to survive, companies have to be able to respond to global trends and economic cycles that are becoming increasingly intense and follow one another ever quicker. With too many permanent contracts a company would become inflexible, and will surely pay the price should the economy or demand decline. Due to the traditional developments this cannot last long.[8]

As freelancers and the collaborating partners form external relations, it makes sense that marketing plays a dominant role in this decision-making process. What is more, the analyses in the platform (usually part of the platform) are important for developing and maintaining optimal customer relations. The ability to effectively respond to the needs and wishes of the visitors/customers determines to a large degree the success of the suppliers on a platform. All these principles are based on marketing.

---

[8] *Source*: Rob Zandbergen, CEO Recruit Gloval staffing (including USG) (Elsevier, 2018).

Due to the functioning in a network and the selling via a platform, the marketing function has to be modified and *upgraded* to management level. This upgrading of marketing means that the member of staff responsible for marketing must have some expertise in the technologies relevant to the network and platform, such as analyses, micro-services (see Chapter 5) and domains. Of course, the 'old' knowledge and skills, such as product knowledge, innovation and services, are also important. And lastly, there has to be knowledge about technological applications at the 'moment of truth', the moment of purchase (whether online or offline). The integration of direct response, direct messaging and the smartphone is essential. This allows direct support to be given at the moment of purchasing, both online and offline.

Without any adaptations by the organisation, systems and decision-making process, the application of a platform and the function in a network will not be successful.

> According to Sana, increasingly more organisations are focusing on e-commerce in order to remain competitive, increase the sales volume and improve the customer experience. They feel the increasing pressure from online competitors, says CEO and managing partner Michiel Schipperus. In order to successfully stay on top of this challenge he believes that organisations should use their e-commerce system not only as an extra sales channel. It is important, for example, that online sales are integrated with other internal systems, such as the ERP system, he suggests. 'It's the only way to stay in the race with your competition.'[9]

A focus on customers is far from easy; it requires an adaptation of all facets of an organisation. Platforms are disruptive due to the commodification: the value that is attached to a platform by the handling, selecting and matching that provides added value for visitors (customers) and suppliers. The platforms are based on collaboration, network effects and technology. As the range of products and services becomes increasingly wider, platforms are disruptive for traditional organisations and market

---

[9] *Source:* https://retailtrends.nl/nieuws/54199/helft-van-b2b-spelers-levert-ook-aan-de-consument?utm_source=email&utm_medium=nieuwsbrief&utm_campaign=RN.

structures. Adaptation is a necessity. This can be done by joining a traditional platform, often aggregators, by developing a platform oneself with other providers or by challenging these platforms as a niche player. An organisation has to choose from one of these three basic strategies. There are plenty of examples of where this had not been done, resulting in the decline or even complete disappearance of an organisation or product. Nokia and Kodak are perfect examples of this. Just take a walk around your local shopping centre and you can see the same thing, empty shops.

Bibliography

Choudary, S. P. (2015). *Platform Scale*. Platform Thinking Labs.

Chapter 5

Networks Become the Competition

Amazon was the first seller on the Internet that enabled other websites to be linked to its own website. This made it possible for providers to sell their products via Amazon; Amazon would then receive commission, a small percentage of the sales price, if the sale was successful. This link was a form of affinity marketing.[1] It is this affinity that is extremely important for platforms. Visitors feel a certain bond with a platform and have their own preferences for a particular proposition.

The Bijenkorf department store in the Netherlands has a clear affinity concept where experience, feeling and hedonism help to bond the target group and form part of the proposition, both online and offline. Amazon was the first to bond customers with affinity concepts on the Internet. This was in fact the beginning of the network economy on the Internet. In its early years, Amazon was a popular website that mainly sold books. In addition to affinity (feeling and hedonism), it also developed an

---

[1]Affinity marketing is a concept that consists of a partnership between a company (supplier) and an organisation that collects people who share the same interests (known as an affinity group) in order to bring a larger number of customers to their service, product or website.

affiliate concept that allowed other websites to be linked with Amazon. The aggregator concept, described earlier, later developed from this. A clear product with a straightforward product code, based on the company's own PIMs system, made linking simple. The link with the Amazon process was a clear win–win situation for everyone.[2] Amazon wanted to have more visitors on its site, while other providers, both small providers as well as publishers, were looking for a sales channel for their products. This formed the basis of Amazon's growth and the power based on an integrated classic sales model.

From the very beginning, Jeff Bezos had a clear vision of the Internet and the ambition to develop Amazon into a global player. Profits were secondary to growth; it was all about expected future profits (value creation) based on the market position. Collaborations, too, were and are part of his growth ambitions. Since the start in 1994, he had set out a number of commercial principles that formed the basis of this collaboration (1999). They are as follows:

- All collaborations have to contribute to the growth in the number of visitors, the number of offers and the number of products in order to ensure customers returned (retention). Achieving a large number of visitors was the goal. In 2017, Amazon had 197 million visitors per month, compared with the monthly 117 million visitors of Walmart. The latest figures for 2018 show over 310 million active Amazon customers.
- An increase in market share was seen due to the loyalty of customers and the increase in the number of customers who had switched from another webshop or a physical provider.
- Access to new markets and new distribution channels — Acquisitions in Germany and Great Britain have increased Amazon's access to these markets.
- Offer new products. The range of products was increased every year. The auction also contributed to more products and more visitors. The auction initiative was launched in 1999, but eBay proved too strong,

---

[2]The title *Business the Amazon.com Way* (1999), Capstone Publishing, Oxford, gives a vivid description of the vision and early years of Amazon.com.

Clothing and shoes (fashion)

Home and kitchen

Travel and tourism

Books/music

Electronics

Sport articles

Automotive parts

Education

Figure 1.   Popular items sold on internet.

leading in 2000 to the change to Amazon Marketplace. Currently, 562 million products are being offered (see Figure 1).[3]

- Respond to changes. Constant modifications are made to systems by making use of the rapid (technological) changes on the Internet. Through this adoption of new developments, Amazon also became a leader in the application of new technologies.
- Discover new products and technologies, and innovate. Acquisitions of start-ups, applying sophisticated analysis systems in order to have an ever better idea of the buying behaviour of groups and individuals to be able to prepare a specific response.
- Reduce competition. If you cannot buy a competitor, you need to look for more effective ways of fending them off. The new competitive relationships will be discussed in Chapter 6.
- Strengthen reputation or further develop credibility.
- Respond to economic changes. Knowledge of customer behaviour is particularly important here as is the active use of media. This knowledge allows media to be used more effectively. By regularly announcing new developments and innovations, there is a constant flow of news that the media can report.

---

[3] *Source*: www.scrapehero.com/many-products-amazon-sell-january-2018/.

The Development of Marketplaces (Sales-Based Platforms)

In 2000, the Amazon website was opened up for other providers who could sell their own products alongside the regular Amazon products that were sold. Amazon received a commission for this. In 2018, these third-party sales actually exceeded the sales of Amazon's own products (53% third-party sales compared with Amazon's 47%). A total of 2 million providers sold their products in this way. This makes these sales, together with Amazon web services, currently the most important generators of turnover and profit. Already in the 1990s, Amazon had, and still has, a strong focus on attracting visitors. Since 2010, Bol.com in the Netherlands has been offering the same facility under the name of Bol Plaza. These days the external parties are integrated in the total product range of Bol.com. A separate Plaza is now no longer necessary. Bol.com is the 'portal' to the market and is linked to suppliers via an order-to-pay process. This was initially based on an EDI link; these days this is an API interface. The processing is carried out through a third party as are the logistics, order handling as well as the payment (*procurement*). Bol.com does, however, have control over the purchasing and the order processes. As already indicated in the definitions, this is an example of a marketplace for sellers.

> Bol.com outsources practically all processes: Bol.com buyers handle the purchasing, and for all subsequent processes the company works with external suppliers, fulfilment partners and delivery services. The webshop offers well over 7 million articles and does business with hundreds of suppliers. This makes it a complex chain with a great many players. 'We want to be in control of the chain ourselves. Transparency and clear communication are necessary for this,' says Harm Jans, Way of working manager, whose team is charged with bringing about structural improvements to the delivery reliability.[4]

Competitive strength in the first phase of networks includes the following:

---

[4] *Source: Supply Chain Magazine*, 1 November 2013.

- large range of products;
- many visitors;
- services, direct contacts;
- direct communication;
- knowledge of search and purchasing processes;
- competitive prices.

Portals, affiliates, exchanges and marketplaces are typical applications in the first phase of the development of the network economy. There is increasingly often a link (the network) and services for one party, usually the sellers. This development accelerated particularly after 2014, due to there being a link between at least two market parties link based on sales opportunities and a link based on buying possibilities. These providers would, as an independent party, sell network facilities to both sides of the market. Marketing was carried out by these two-sided or multisided platforms to attract visitors. The facilities offered were a consequence of a realised sale, such as logistics (home deliveries), payment facilities, analyses, web support and customer care. Examples of this are as follows:

- Takeaway.com — home deliveries of meals from local restaurants.
- Booking.com — for booking hotel rooms or holiday accommodation.
- Airbnb — for renting rooms or accommodation from private individuals.

All these parties make use of network facilities and create network effects. This makes the new party the centre of a network, and thereby a new powerful market party. It is practically impossible to compete with such a network. It is therefore participate or perish. The criticisms levelled at Uber, Airbnb, Thuisbezorgd and many others are based on this. The power of these platforms lies in the dominant market position, the extent of the range of products and/or services and the number of consumers (an interaction) and the return behaviour.

The new multisided networks are no longer based on the facilitation of a single party (for the sales), but on the facilitation of the wishes of various parties (consumers and (service) providers). This is when the network responds by facilitating the needs of consumers by offering a multitude of needs-related services. That's why there is no two-sided platform (linking consumers and providers), but a multisided platform, whereby a large variety of consumer needs is linked to many providers. Communication and interaction between the parties form the core of the business model.

Competitive strength of multisided platforms is as follows:

- large supply due to network connections;
- complete range of services;
- matching based on needs and selection of the supply;
- engagement by both the customers and the providers;
- many visitors;
- different revenue models (not only transactions);
- specific algorithms created on the basis of experience;
- communication and interaction between all parties involved (supply and demand, information and sales).

Development of the Competitive Strength of a Network Economy

- *Phase 1: Linking websites through affiliate possibilities*
  - ○ Grouping websites in a portal;
  - ○ Grouping the supply with a large party such as Amazon or Bol.com;
  - ○ Making markets transparent through exchanges and connecting consumers with providers (via API).

- *Phase 2: Applications with independent marketplaces, sales-oriented*
  - ○ Facilitating one party in the market usually via information (*infomediaries*[5]), such as with many health platforms: information on health issues and a link to a possible provider.
  - ○ Also themed marketplaces that, on the basis of needs and information, have links to providers, such as those seen in sports websites.

---

[5]An *infomediary* is a website that provides specific information on behalf of providers based on questions. It can involve both products and services. This term is an amalgamation of the words information and intermediary.

- *Phase 3: Multisided platforms operate on the basis of matching needs with facilities*
  - o These platforms operate on the basis of matching needs with product/service solutions. In addition, related products and services are offered that can be part of this choice or needs. These platforms link supply and user information of many providers and match these with a specific demand. Examples include Airbnb, for the demand for short-term accommodation and Uber, for transport.
  - o Both sides of the market are linked here through the matching function and a connection based on APIs (*interfaces*). In the beginning, we saw this with reservation systems for hotels and restaurants (Opentable.com and Booking.com) and with dating sites, which match potential partners (see Figure 2).
- *Phase 4: Further developments of network applications such as blockchain and bitcoins*
  - o With blockchain and bitcoins, no links are made. Instead, the network is used for distributed recording (such as with blockchain) or distributed value components based on use, such as with bitcoins. The network is no longer a collection of linked independent units, but is a unit consisting of independently connected components (nodes). The network in its entirety is the entity in the market. The strength of these networks largely depends on the participating parties. Similar networks as an independent entity will compete with one another.

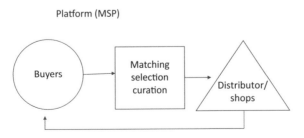

Figure 2.   The core of a multisided platform: The matching module.

Is the Success of a Platform Based on Customer Behaviour?

With traditional organisational structures, the customer is the endpoint. Customers are never informed about the consequences of complaints or an organisation's learning experience. At the very most, the complaint is handled and the customer is later asked whether he or she is satisfied. The customer doesn't receive any feedback about the fact that the cause of complaints often lies with the organisation and that complaints occur frequently, and therefore, an adjustment of the personnel, processes or structures is necessary. It is often also not possible to contact an organisation. The telephone number and email address are often well-hidden on a website or not provided there at all. This shortcoming can be resolved by an FAQ, a prepared questionnaire. At the end, the customer is asked whether the answer was of any help.

With a multisided platform, the customer forms the basis. The strategy is aimed at acquiring and retaining customers as they form a platform's competitive strength. A constant analysis of customer behaviour is necessary for success. The long-standing RFM analysis from Direct Marketing is still a good basis for these platforms:

> RFM is a method used for analysing customer value. It is commonly used in database marketing and direct marketing and has received particular attention in retail and professional services industries.
>
> **RFM** stands for the following three dimensions:
>
> > **R**ecency — How recently did the customer purchase?
> >
> > **F**requency — How often do they purchase?
> >
> > **M**onetary value — How much do they spend?
>
> Customer purchases may be represented by a table with columns for the customer name, date of purchase and purchase value. One approach to RFM is to assign a score for each dimension on a scale from 1 to 10. The maximum score represents the preferred behaviour and a formula could be used to calculate the three scores for each customer.[6]

---

[6] *Source*: https://en.wikipedia.org/wiki/RFM_(customer_value).

By regularly carrying out the RFM analysis, companies gain knowledge about the customer base and the loyalty of each individual customer. Historical comparisons give insights into the vitality of the customer base and the degree of loyalty per customer. The RFM module is also used for predictive modelling. Based on this analysis, predictions can be made regarding the total customer base (turnover, customer loss) and at an individual customer level, so that targeted communication can be carried out. RFM can be part of the analyses that lead to an algorithm. Often other indicators, however, are also determined that say more about loyalty. Good matches determine the website's success and customer satisfaction.

> People used to always shop in their own town or neighbourhood. But now through websites people have access to products from all over the world. The most important criteria for buying online is, in fact, the unlimited supply and the good proposition (match).

Further Developments and Modifications of the Competition Model

After the Internet bubble burst at the start of this century, there arose a greater sense of realism about the power of the Internet. The acceptance of Internet applications had no bubble and continued to grow steadily in all those years (see Table 1).

The Netherlands was an early adopter when it came to the application of the Internet. KPN, which was the first telecom company to be privatised, had a major role in this. There was a high cable density, in part thanks to the flat landscape and soft ground, which made it easier to lay cables under the surface. In 2000, some 70% of the Dutch population were already using the Internet — at home (60%) as well as at work (52%) and for study purposes (40%).[7] This, of course, includes some double counting.

---

[7] www.cbs.nl/nl-nl/nieuws/2005/24/dertig-procent-van-de-volwassenen-internet-niet, 2005.

Table 1.   Internet penetration worldwide.

	%
Worldwide	60
North Europe	95
West Europe	92
USA	88.7 (285 million); 52.2 by mobile phone
Asia Pacific	63
China	63 (900 million); 75 by mobile phone

The Internet was used at work, as well as privately, to shop (web-shops), to communicate (email, chat rooms and video) and to search for information. The development of the infrastructural function of the Internet really took off only after the introduction of the smartphone, which enabled everyone to be accessible everywhere and at all times.

The use of the smartphone and the rapid acceptance of applications of the Internet resulted in increasingly more possibilities that fitted in with people's normal behaviour when it came to communicating and sharing information.

The year 2004 saw the introduction of Thefacebook.com, which was later renamed Facebook.com. In its first 2 years, it was a communication and matching site for students, but after 2006, this restriction was lifted and Facebook was ready for an explosive growth to 3.5 billion users in 2018.

The increasing use of the Internet can perhaps best be seen from the usage figures of Google Search, Google's search engine. In the course of 17 years, the number of searches increased by 200,000% — from 14 billion in 2000, through 1.2 trillion in 2012, to over 3 trillion in 2017. It should be noted here that the number of searches carried out on smartphones has grown rapidly over the last few years, while the number of searches using a desktop computer has decreased. The overall number of searches has, however, continued to rise, particularly among large dominant market parties such as Amazon.com. Alongside Google Search, the services have expanded rapidly, in particular due to the connection with the smartphone and location-based services.

Since 2004, there have been a number of significant developments. It became increasingly difficult to compete against market leaders. This led to a convergence due to independent providers looking to connect with these market leaders, as we saw with marketplaces.

- Providers began to increasingly operate internationally in order to take advantage of economies of scale as well as of the growth possibilities of markets that were lagging behind, relatively speaking.
- Market reach was the basis for rapid growth.
- Independent providers offered a particular facility to bond consumers and providers. This occurred in three specific areas: supply of companies (such as portals), supply of products (via marketplaces and market leaders) and supply of information (via search engines and specific sites).

In addition, based on the network strategy, links were made in three areas of application as follows:

- links based on search criteria;
- links based on products/services;
- links based on facilities;
- links based on registration.

New Competition: Google

Through the Google search engine, links were made to companies that met the search criteria. The search engine came up with a hit list of websites, after which you could click on a particular one. Companies developed programs to enable them to achieve a high score with the use of a particular search key (SEO). The challenge was to be listed among the first 10, in other words on the first page of the search results. This meant that you had to take the search algorithms into account and design your website in such a way that the algorithm would give it a high valuation on the basis of the search results. Specialised agencies ensured that websites would achieve ever better scores. The strategy of search engine optimisation, SEO, became an important competitive factor that helped companies to be found and chosen by potential customers. If the ranking was still too low, companies could always buy a high mention via AdWords, a paid listing when certain search keys were used. Increasingly, often this did not involve a link to a website, but to a product page on the website. The competition with Google took place on the basis of findability, ranking and the listing of the website (directly linked).

Search criteria became a new competition weapon. Google is a specific search engine for finding information on the Internet. This is not restricted to just products, but can involve a huge variety of information. As described earlier, searching for and finding products is an important commercial activity. However, if you already know where you are going to buy, why would you use a general search engine? You could also look for the product directly from the provider: the producer/supplier, the distributor/webshop. Certainly, if you already trust the brand or the webshop, this would make more sense. Many searches take place directly with Amazon, Bol.com and Coolblue, as well as with Booking.com. Google.com therefore, quite rightly says in its defence to the European Union that the market share for 'searching' is much smaller than is currently thought. These providers facilitate the search and enable customers to buy directly.

> As of early 2017, Amazon has become the top place consumers go on the Internet to search for products. In a Raymond James study published in early 2017, 52% of people said that Amazon is now their first choice for product searches. A 2016 BloomReach study found that the percentage of people who start online searches for products on Amazon is even higher — at 55% — while Google's share of product search has dropped to about 28%. This continues a more than three-year growth trend for Amazon, suggesting that their share of product searches will continue to grow.[8]

Google's decreasing dominance of only searching led to the introduction of a new Google facility: Google Shopping. Launched in 2012, Google Shopping was a Google service that allowed users to search for products that were sold on websites for online shopping and to compare the prices of the various suppliers. The advantage for the searcher is a direct link between

---

[8] *Source*: www.digitaldougnut.com, Brian Beck, 21 November 2017. https://retailtrends.nl/nieuws/54199/helft-van-b2b-spelers-levert-ook-aan-de-consument?utm_source=email&utm_medium=nieuwsbrief&utm_campaign=RN.

the search query and the product (not supplier). This way, Google created a new revenue model based on a commission on any sales (and listing).

Originally, the prices shown on Google Shopping were based on the data from the sellers. Income was generated through AdWords advertisements as well as other Google services. In May 2012, however, Google announced that the search for products service (which was renamed Google Shopping) would shift at the end of 2012 to a paid model whereby the companies would have to pay for any listing of their products or services. This led to the creation of a new dimension, whereby products were offered via a search model. In addition to SEO, providers now also had the option of offering their products via Google Shopping. This was a new Google platform where providers and consumers were matched at the product level. Google Shopping was always visible with every match, thereby creating a different form of competition. Competition was no longer based on the ranking of the search results, but based on other providers using Google Shopping. Not being on Google Shopping meant that the company became irrelevant on this service. This led, of course, to irritation among those providers taking part in Google Shopping. They continued to compete on the basis of the 'old' system — SEO.

Customers' search choices became a competitive factor that had the following consequences for providers:

- competition through a provider's own business model, physical and via their own website;
- competition based on search criteria (SEO);
- competition through the Google Shopping platform at the product level was new. This made it possible for products to be sold directly to buyers without the need for extra marketing efforts.

The old distribution channel came under pressure as suppliers were now able to offer products directly through Google Search and later Google Shopping. The strength of this development and of this competition only became clear when the European Union carried out studies into unfair competition. This study was conducted in response to complaints from providers who did not take part, or did not wish to participate, in Google Shopping. The illusion arose that the ranking could be influenced, and through Google

Shopping, the power shifted towards Google. This led in June 2017 to Google receiving a fine from the European Union of €2.4 billion, as Google Shopping was listed as a top priority in the search engine. This was a defensive ruling, which made a new vision on platforms necessary. Moreover, it was a clear indication of the competitive strength of platforms and the lethargic attitude of European companies towards this development. The competitive environment was changing very quickly. Banning was a desperate response from the European Union and the providers who had waited too long to introduce any new competitive strategy. However, despite the fine imposed upon Google, the competition was to change radically due to the impact of the network economy and other forces. Google was the first provider to recognise the competitive strength of networks. Companies therefore had to take serious account of the Google ranking. What's more, a direct link at the product level was possible, changing the distributor's role as a result. Shops, dealers and distributors had proven their worth in the physical supply chain, but now increasingly faced various problems.

> The introduction of Google Shopping meant just one thing for companies across the B2C and B2B spectrum — retailers, brands, manufacturers, and distributors — not being listed on Amazon creates risk of obscurity and irrelevance for the companies. The rate of return on "traditional" Internet marketing methods for products — using Search Engine Optimization and Paid Search tactics to drive traffic to products on a branded website experience — is decaying. Yes, branded product websites remain relevant and can still provide a powerful customer experience. However, they are simply not the engine for product discovery and purchases they once were.[9]

Is a Network the Basis for a New Competition Strategy?

Another provider that links supply to websites is, for example, Thuisbezorgd. Active since 2000 and now part of Takeaway.com, it is an important player in the home delivery market for meals. In Europe, there are currently 33,000 restaurants affiliated with Takeway.com. The company operates in nine countries. In the last year, Takeaway.com has processed more than

---

[9] *Source*: www.digitaldoughnut.com, David Beck, 21 November 2017.

68 million orders for 11.5 million customers. With Thuisbezorgd, the Netherlands is the most important with 7500 affiliated residents, good for a total of €550 million worth of orders (in 2017). This makes Thuisbezorgd by far the largest order site in the Netherlands. For this link, restaurants pay a 13% commission, but receive an average of €80,000 in return. This is often around 60–80% of their turnover. Not using the platform is no longer an option. Thuisbezorgd is a typical multisided platform, where the supply of restaurants is linked to the demand of customers (based on the possibilities offered by a network). The following step may undoubtedly involve further refinements through direct links at the product level. The competitive strength of Thuisbezorgd is such that there is no serious second provider or any independent restaurant that can develop a similar proposition at the national and international levels.

The Booking.com model has also become a success (Figure 3). Initially a site for hotel reservations, and then later also for offering other possibilities such as holiday homes and apartments, Booking.com was set up in 1995 in the Netherlands. Its real growth, however, began after 2005 when it was taken over by the American company Priceline.com and shortly afterwards merged with ActiveHotels.com. Booking.com is an intermediary and facilitates the reservations of rooms, apartments and homes. The providers take care of the information and photos. These are not verified by Booking.com, not only in view of the latter's position as an independent intermediary but also due to the wide range of available accommodation. Each day, Booking.com processes some 1.5 million reservations. The profit last year was €2.4 billion. During a recent stay in Nepal, the hotel owner informed me that he received 70% of his reservations through Booking.com. Alongside Booking.com, Airbnb and Uber help to form the basis of the sharing economy. In all cases, this leads to a different form of competition in the various markets as well as to irritation among traditional providers who are not able to compete against this competition.

Effect on the Product Supply: New Providers Lead to New Competition

Large providers also communicated in other markets and made use of the possibilities of online connections. Initially, there was no network, but

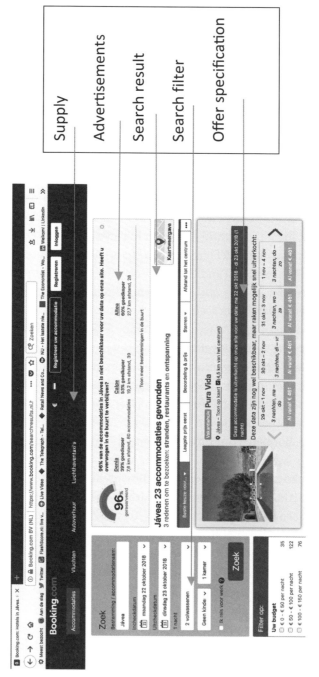

Figure 3.   Website of booking.com.

rather a multipoint connection — many connections to a central point, the supplier's website. A speedy penetration in many markets was possible. This helped these providers to disrupt the market as they began to compete as a new entrant with different prices. The margins of the traditional parties came under pressure, as did their services and turnover. Amazon in particular led the way, also in the area of technology. This was a new form of competition where Amazon competed with new resources. Amazon disrupted the retail sector and the supply chain, particularly in the US, Germany and Great Britain; Amazon wanted to first of all gain market leadership through acquisitions and aggressive growth and to attack traditional providers. The motto was as follows: *We are after your profit in whatever market you are.*[10] They succeeded. The traditional parties were simply too slow in adjusting and in their technological applications of the Internet. What's more, collaboration between various parties is difficult to achieve also on the Internet. Joining the market leader (aggregator) is simpler and not disruptive to the traditional business model. The convergence led to marketplaces (portals) where providers could sell their products. The marketplace took over the marketing and advertising. There was still the old supply paradigm, selling products.

Through the bundling of marketing strength, the new market leaders were able to offer an alternative to traditional providers. Through the bundling of the supply, the position of these market leaders was reinforced without undermining the traditional business model of the affiliated providers. Online marketing and sales were handed over to the new market leaders, the platforms. This led to a reduction in costs, as use could also be made of the supporting services such as logistics and payment facilities. The independent competitive battle shifted towards a collective competitive battle by the market leader (such as Amazon, Airbnb, Alibaba) against the classic providers. If companies clung onto the old business model and competition model, this would become an unequal competitive battle.

A percentage of the turnover of course had to be paid, usually between 10% and 20%. There were also fixed costs such as connection, advertising and subscription costs. But in return there were also savings in marketing, sales and advertising costs.

---

[10]Study trip in 2015 at a meeting of Amazon analysts.

What Effect Does the Matching on a Platform Have on the Demand and Supply?

At the heart of a platform lies the matching module that links the consumer's need to the provider's range of products and services. On the basis of this need, the platform searches for products that best suit it and then ranks them. Only then will the supplier be visible, but not necessarily if the platform is the contracting party. Platforms that only show websites of suppliers belong to the first phase, based on affinity.

On the basis of the matching, a match filter is put together.

What is the Impact on the Supply Chain?

All these examples are based on applications aimed at the end user, particularly consumers. These developments are of course also taking place in the B2B market. Alibaba, Amazon and Google have special sites and propositions for this market, where companies can or must buy articles in bulk and links are set up between manufacturers and companies for specific customised products, tendering or services. When it comes to the purchasing of standard products, these companies therefore become wholesalers. The major difference is the market scope. Using a configurator, the specific wishes of a consumer are translated into a product order, which is linked to the machines. The Internet takes over the role of handling the specific order.

In addition, the functions are tested for relevance. As a result, companies will change and functions will be modified. The change from a linear supply chain to a supply chain based on a network ecosystem is an example of this.

Platforms in the Supply Chain

The development of platforms in the supply chain began already at the start of this century (2000–2001). In the B2B market, the number of providers and consumers is limited, but they are often known by the market parties. The role of the providers and consumers in a supply chain is very specific. It can even be unique as tailor-made solutions are offered. Many activities, however, are generic, such as logistics, procurement and marketing. It is by bundling these generic activities in a virtual marketplace that the role of these parties will change. The independent entity now becomes part of a specific chain, where added value becomes more important than independence. An example of this has long been seen in the construction sector, where contractors are the connecting factor between suppliers and clients. Suppliers are hired on the basis of their connection with the contractor and their specific expertise. This was also the basic principle behind the development of B2B exchanges. A form of platform that connects the consumer with the supplier. One of the first applications was the build-to-order model whereby the consumer, through all sorts of EDI links, made a direct connection with the supplier. Based on the EDI, the order was placed directly in the system of the supplier. This was clearly an efficient method, but the EDI link also made it a complex and expensive one. The Internet provided the solution for a better way, by putting, for example, the catalogue of the supplier online. What's more, it was determined in advance with which suppliers business would be conducted. Of course, the suppliers had to meet all sorts of requirements in terms of reliability, product certainty and continuity. This introduced a degree of regulation to the market. Taking part is an opportunity for bringing in orders. Not taking part meant that a supplier has to compete on the free market, which is becoming increasingly difficult.

By constantly placing the potential order at various suppliers with the request to make a quote, a price competition arises between a small number of suppliers. This can not only lead to a tighter bond between the suppliers and the customer but also lead to a cost advantage for that customer.[11]

The model in Figure 4 identifies three focus areas: order handling (demand fulfilment), demand planning and supply planning.

The new intermediaries are based on the communication possibilities of the Internet. These new parties are disruptive in the supply chain and have their own business model. Due to the combination of supply and

---

[11] Scully, A. B. and Woods, W. W. A. (1999). *B2B Exchanges: The Killer Application in the Business-to-Business Internet Revolution.* ISI Publications, p. 24.

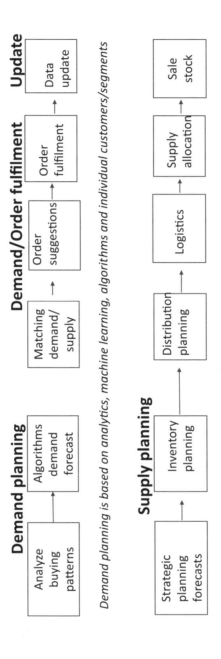

Figure 4.   Standard model for Supply Chain Management.

demand, they are capable of playing an important role in order handling (price) and making the market transparent. This can be done by inviting a limited number of providers to make a quote. This can be done through open auctions for particular assignments or through a tender. In these cases, the intermediary acts on behalf of the consumers in order to realise a good supply and price and for the providers in order to make the demand transparent and to mediate in the sale. The focus of these new parties was on growth. Growth took priority over profit in the short term. One of the first parties that worked on the basis of this strategy was www. shop2gether.com. It was through collecting the smaller orders of often smaller parties that this platform was able to realise good prices from providers. This was one of the first concepts that changed the supply chain. Along with the mediation, increasingly more knowledge of the buying processes and procedures was acquired. It makes sense that this knowledge is one of the value creation components of these new parties. This knowledge often contributes to the value determination of the business and forms the basis for future profits.

The effects that these new entrants had on the supply chain were immediately clear. They are as follows:

- online is cheaper than physical buying, or the old link with system links such as EDI;
- global reach so that foreign parties can also take part in the supply and demand;
- new methods for determining the price (modular and facilitative);
- aggregation of the demand is possible, which leads to a greater negotiating power among consumers;
- transparency in markets.

Examples from these early years are the platforms for transport, raw materials, excess stocks and insurances. Due to the new virtual applications of the intermediaries, the supply chain came under pressure. As a result, they became more efficient and had a positive effect on costs and prices. In addition, the registered information allowed for better analyses to be carried out than was previously possible, both on the demand side and on the supply side.

Table 2.   Disruption through technology.

Online Platform	Most Important Product	Disrupt Industry	Examples of Companies
Apple	iOS mobile platform	PC operating systems	Microsoft
Facebook	Social network	Advertising	Traditional advertising agencies
Uber	Transport on call	Taxi sector	Classic taxi companies and permit system
Airbnb	Private accommodation rental	Hotels and booking sites	Hotel sector and municipalities
Takeaway	Meals delivery service	Restaurants	Restaurants, hotels and bars
Booking.com	Hotel reservation systems	Hotels	Last-minute special deals and hotels
Netflix	Films and programmes on demand	Classic broadcasters	TV-viewing behaviour and advertising revenue
Amazon	Online purchases	Shops/retail	Shops and retail chains and smaller municipalities

There was, of course, a disruptive change which had consequences for the traditional suppliers and traditional supply chain (Table 2). Whereas previously distributors were used (also in this B2B market), there was now the possibility to respond directly to the demand. Additionally, consumers could be approached directly by the suppliers/producers. It was feared that this would have a cannibalisation effect on the traditional distribution channel. For this reason, parties sometimes considered introducing their own platform (exchange) onto the market; however, that was a very defensive move and did not take advantage of the benefits of an independent party. Consumers, too, would then tend to prefer this independent party, leading to the producer having to compete with its own distribution network, which is clearly an undesirable situation.

The exchanges in the various forms at the beginning of this century were the start to a closer collaboration between parties in the supply chain.

Through the application of the Internet, physical restrictions disappear. The stable relationships in markets would in time be affected by this (the traditional chain model). Due to the Internet, the market reach has also increased. In actual fact, products could now be sold anywhere in the world, although in the early years this remained just a theoretical possibility. Based on the traditional relationships, the newcomers — start-ups and foreign suppliers — first had to conquer a market. Through the application of the Internet, there were advantages of the economies of scale, direct communication and a wide range of products and services, but these were advantages within the traditional chain (therefore not disruptive, innovative at the most). There were also disadvantages in relation to the traditional model: the unfamiliarity among buyers, language differences, logistics, local legislation and consumer protection (return of items and privacy). New entrants made use of the strengths of the home market, such as economies of scale and technological lead, which they exported to new markets. Amazon was able to grow quickly abroad (as a webshop) due to its strong position in the United States and the size of its home market. This strategy worked well as long as other markets had not sufficiently advanced in how they used the Internet. Amazon conquered these markets and also wanted to be a market leader straightaway (such as in England and Germany). This growth has stagnated in the last decade as other markets (such as the Netherlands) have undergone rapid developments. The costs involved in conquering these markets quickly rose, while the market leadership had already been achieved by a local party (such as Bol.com). For Amazon, it was clear that this strategy was no longer effective.

China

The new competition from China was based mostly on low prices. The longer delivery times were accepted in view of the large price differences. For China, the Internet turned out to be a catalyst for economic growth. A large home market, low wages and a stable government with a long-term vision ensured for a rapid growth of Internet companies, with Alibaba leading the way. The impact was fairly limited at the start, but Alibaba showed stable growth. It is becoming increasingly clear that Chinese companies have tremendous staying power and use different revenue models. This will help them to disrupt traditional markets in the long run.

These new providers continued to be based on the classic market approach and traditional chains. But they actually only had an impact on shops, who were the first to feel the pain. Physical restrictions, such as location, shop and warehouse space and opening hours disappeared through the application of the Internet. The battle between the old providers that were based on physical foundations against the new online providers that used the possibilities offered by the Internet (the virtual world) was a battle for customer preference. The shift in turnovers and the impact of this shift in specific sectors (such as consumer electronics, books and clothing) showed the purchasing preferences of the customers. The change in the purchasing preferences led, for example, to fewer physical shops, clearly visible in many shopping centres (particularly in municipalities with fewer than 100,000 residents).

Competition in the B2B Market

Particularly in a business environment (B2B), the relationship between supplier and customer/user is important. If we look at pricing in the market, for companies it is important to purchase as economically as possible in order to be able to compete on price. Strong purchasing is essential; lower prices lead to higher margins and/or lower prices for special offers. Savings also lead to better profitability of the activities and assets, as can be seen from the DuPont model.

> In past times purchasing involved bartering. These days the principle still remains much the same transaction that arises from the exchange of a product or service for a monetary consideration. The verbs to 'buy' and to 'sell' have been frequently used throughout history and have gradually been joined by the verb to 'purchase'. These days this activity refers to rational and well considered buying.
>
> **The DuPont model demonstrates that financial successes in the area of purchasing have a direct effect on a company's financial performance.** The profitability of this company is expressed here through the indicator 'return on equity'. This indicator shows how effectively the equity is used. The DuPont model illustrates the relationship between the balance sheet and profit and loss account, and provides insight into how the profit has

been realised. With any reductions of the costs, and therefore the purchasing prices, the profit margin is positively affected and therefore also the profitability.[12]

It is through new forms such as 'auctions', 'portals' and 'tendering' that transparency arises. Also, another form of competition is created, one that is much sharper. Often one has to negotiate with unknown providers and unknown suppliers. By competing on the end market, the loyalty will also decrease. Foreign providers are disrupting the negotiating power of suppliers. Also the possibility of purchasing product parts from specialists and assembling them into a single product is a new form of competition, a modular approach to products and services based on network connections. Consumers negotiate separately for each component. An iPhone, for example, contains many Samsung components, but the company competes at the end-product level. This approach has become particularly clear through Brexit and the tariffs America is imposing upon imports. There has been a naive focus on end products, while product parts still have to be assembled or have just been assembled. This may be outside America with products from other countries, as well as with American components.

Economies of Scale and Competition

I have previously suggested that Porter's model is not sufficient for determining a competition strategy. This is to do with the assumptions that Porter makes about the market. In Porter's model, the supply chain is regarded as linear and assumes that competitive advantages can be achieved through economies of scale and by protecting the market from competition (Van Alstyne *et al.*, 2016). Porter argues that a market is attractive if you are one of the few producers, if there is little competition, if the buyers and suppliers have little power and if there are few replacement products, and also if there are high barriers for entry. In other words, Porter says that success in the market and its attractiveness largely depend on competition with other providers. Advantages are mainly

---

[12] *Source*: https://facto.nl/dupont-model-in-2016-springlevend/?vakmedianet-approve-cookies=1&_ga=2.36594211.2022132233.1539177209-1236589040.1538667374.

gained through cost reductions, which give rise to *comparative price advantages*.

In these supply chains, all the products were comparable (there was no *mass customisation* yet), and the competitive strengths were as follows: how cheaply could the company produce, what quantity could the company produce and is the company the only one that can produce this as cheaply and has comparative price advantages through cost saving.

Many markets, both consumer markets and B2B as well as industrial markets, are changing under the influence of the applications of online platforms and networks. The traditional strategy is usually still based on the classic model of supply chains and market position, whereby the technology is applied in the customer relationships only to a limited degree. In the classic approach, the technology ensures for a more efficient business model (doing digital), not for change. This leads to efficiency advantages, not to a defensible competitive advantage. In the traditional developments, the technology forms the basis of the business model (being digital). In this sense, the technological possibilities, such as networks and collaboration in platforms, lie at the heart of the competitive strength. In the traditional business models and market structures, there is a lack of digitalisation and sensoring, a constant monitoring of disruptions, which are typical in the network approach. The analysis of customer behaviour and loyalty, as already described, ensures closer customer relationships. This will be examined in more detail in Chapter 6. If there is insufficient adoption of the new possibilities, traditional companies will come evermore under pressure.

Competition Arises between Networks: Providers Compete within a Network

Large Internet providers such as Amazon were at the origins of the disruption in markets. These aggregators made it possible for smaller providers to also sell via the Internet. They were able to take advantage of the popularity of these websites and make use of the facilities. This formed the basis for the further development of platforms and the change in markets. Traditional providers do, however, need to change and reconsider what the best strategy is for them: joining an aggregator, developing a new concept themselves such as a platform, joining a traditional network or instead focusing on the added value they can provide as a niche player.

Data, analyses and algorithms form the basis for contacts with customers and for communication. Technology facilitates, but doing nothing is not an option.

Algorithms determine to a large degree the competitive battle within the platform, while platforms/networks compete against one another for visitors. The technology behind the platform is of crucial importance for the success of the network.

Bibliography

Van Alstyne, M. W., Parker, G., and Choudary, S. P. (2016). Pipelines, platforms, and the new rules of strategy, *Harvard Business Review*, April.

Chapter 6

Technology as a Basis for New Competitive Relationships

Technology is becoming increasingly more important in the competitive battle; this applies not only to systems and links but also to algorithms. The adage 'first mover takes all' still very much applies, with the first application getting the highest market share. The traditional developments, which are based on the application of technology, not only take place in a specific market but are also quickly copied into other markets and other applications. Technological, marketing and business applications are important in order to jointly determine the proposition. The following three developments can be identified here:

- technological applications in relation to the market;
- technological applications in the product;
- technological applications in the infrastructure.

What is the Relationship with a Market?

The technological applications in relation to the market are most noticeable with the end users. These applications include virtual reality, augmented reality, artificial reality, along with sensoring systems and location-based technology, which supports the moment of attention (or purchase). Track-and-tracing provides a better overview of the logistics, and cameras linked to the Internet offer new security possibilities. These applications are notable, yet do not change the product or infrastructure. These applications are often quickly followed by sophisticated applications with the same (functional) purpose. This makes it appear as if the technological developments are advancing rapidly, but are just the outer layers of applications that make use of networks.

What are the Technological Applications in Products?

New products show a specific technical application. Technology forms an integral part of the product, for example, in cars, computers, cameras, television and much more. Through these sophisticated applications, the products are becoming increasingly complex and offer the user more and more facilities. The product's life is no longer related to its technical life, but rather its economic life. The latest technological possibilities are applied, leading to products becoming outdated, as can be seen with smartphones. This is, of course, an economic stimulus for the suppliers of smartphones such as Apple and Samsung, but also for all suppliers.

As suggested previously, the application of technology does not lead to a long-term competitive advantage. The advantage is short lived. Other providers will quickly integrate the same applications or come up with better ones. This leads to a competitive battle between market leaders, who have the advantage of many users and the necessary resources to invest in innovations. The market is largely driven by a small number of providers. This can be seen with smartphones and computers, as well as with other providers of electronics.

> Google Assistant interpreted. The speaker can answer questions and carry out tasks such as playing music, keeping a diary and ordering shopping. In the United States and Great Britain, the competitor of Amazon's Echo has been available for some time now. As the device could not understand Dutch, the speaker has not been sold in the Netherlands

as yet. The speakers will be available in Dutch stores as of 24 October, but can now already be ordered. Google Home costs 149 euros and Google Home Mini 59 euros.[1]

Adjusting the Infrastructure

The most recent application involves changing the infrastructure. Fast Internet, fibre optics and 5G are changes in the infrastructure that make new applications possible. There are also other developments that have a facilitative effect, such as cloud computing, VPN, virtual private networks, blockchain and platforms. These developments ensure for a better and faster infrastructure, also for specific possibilities on which applications have been based. These developments have a significant impact on competition, which are as follows:

- you have to participate, otherwise other providers take over your market position;
- you have to take part because customers want this;
- you have to take part to keep the profitability of operations intact.

This can be clearly seen with physical shops and providers who operate through physical shops. For too long, the customers' changing wishes and their different buying behaviour were downplayed, making it difficult to respond on time to the new possibilities of the infrastructure (the Internet). As the old providers and market leaders were not alert enough to respond to these changes, they lost a great deal of their market share to the new market leaders on the Internet. Obvious examples are department stores. Only in England, 30% of the department stores went out of business since 2010, others are still struggling. Compare the old department stores with the new aggregators, department stores, like Amazon, JD.com or Alibaba and you can see how rapidly the market is changing.

---

[1] *Source*: https://retailtrends.nl/nieuws/54198/google-home-te-koop-in-nederland-ook-bij-albert-heijn.

Is the Speed of Change Important?

You often hear about the speed of the changes, making it practically impossible to follow and implement the technological developments. This is simply not true. The technological applications are based on a particular strategy. And you cannot change a strategy every year. The strategy is carried out to achieve a particular goal. This goal is fixed as is the organisation and organisational culture, as well as many of the resources. It is on this basis that a strategy is determined and executed, and to which various technological tools contribute. At the heart of the technological tools, as described previously, are the fixed tools, which are sometimes stable within particular limits, such as the infrastructure, and are sometimes more dynamic such as in relation with the market. There are also often financial limitations in the ability to innovate. This may be due to a shrinking profit margin or a strong focus on profitability (instead of value creation). And it is through this latter application, the relationship with the market, that the feeling arises of it all going so quickly. The new applications of the technology, however, are often an improvement to the old application; the function remains intact. This may sound a little cryptic, but it means that on the basis of the function and envisaged goals, the most appropriate technology is used. The technological changes make it appear as if this is all going very quickly; however, from a functional point of view this is not really the case. What is the great change between a landline telephone, the old Nokia mobile phone and a smartphone? Not much has changed really as far as the telephone function is concerned. In the application, however, a great deal has changed. The Nokia phone became a mobile phone and the smartphone added many new possibilities for the user (individually determined).

- Is a website really that much different than the old leaflet or brochure? The reach is different, but the function remains the same.
- Is not a webshop a copy of the old shop where the physical has simply been replaced by the virtual? It is for good reason that we refer to a multichannel, two separate channels that only differ in terms of the applied infrastructure. It is only in recent years that new applications have been sought.

- Is not a platform a type of shopping centre?
- Is not a multisided platform similar to a magazine with subscribers (visitors) and advertisers? And is not this also the case with trade fairs and trade shows?
- Is not a multisided platform the same as these old concepts, but with a new infrastructure? It is essentially the same at its core; the use of the application may change, but the function of the application remains the same. (As with the difference between paying by entering your PIN and contactless payment, the payment function remains intact.) New payment systems like Ayden, Alipay or Google pay make use of the latest technology and convenience for the users. Amazon already employed a few years the one-click-payment-system, which involves genuine contactless payment. The technology is not new, but with the application you have to compete with all those other providers that offer the same. Back in 1994, Michael Tracy already suggested that the application of technology only leads to a small competitive advantage, which would quickly even itself out. Adopting new technology is not an option, it is a necessity.

What are the New IT Possibilities?

For the classic organisation a specific system support could be applied that contributed to the efficiency of the organisation. This was often the so-called enterprise resource planning (ERP) systems; large and static, they were data warehouses that stored the information for various applications within an organisation. These systems supported all (linear) operational processes ensuring there was greater control over the various processes and the mutual connection between processes and functions. Modifications were complex, time consuming and expensive. For competition on dynamic markets this sort of organisation is too sluggish to be able to respond to new competitive relationships, new technologies and the different customer behaviour. Products and services have to change along with the wishes of customers. Speed is then essential for competitive strength.

Figure 1 is an example system set-up for microservices.

The flexibility of the infrastructure determines the choice of technology. Various systems and programming technologies can be chosen from this. The communication can involve either the simple transfer of data

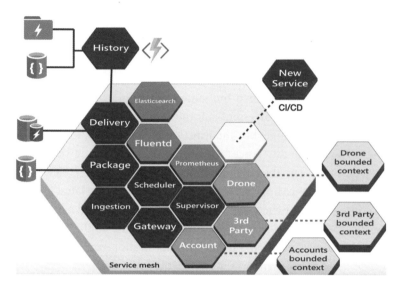

Figure 1. (Microsoft Azure). Example system set-up for microservices, separate units linked to one another.

(which happened with EDI) or two or more services that are connected to one another (synchronisation). The consumer layer is the point at which consumers (human users, other services or third parties) communicate with the system, whereas a provider layer (suppliers) consists of all the services that have been defined. These days microservices have been chosen for such applications.

Microservices are a software development technique, a variant of the service-oriented architecture (SOA) architectural style that structures an application as a collection of loosely coupled services. In a microservices architecture, services are fine grained and the protocols are lightweight.[2]

Microservices are separate units, which have a particular function and have a program written for them. Through the coupling of many of these microservices an algorithm is created, which jointly carries out a particular function. This algorithm consists of a series of standard microservices and specific microservices for the application. The function can be

---

[2] *Source*: Wikipedia.

modified by either adding or removing a microservice. Many software firms have a library with standard microservices that can be applied. This enables much quicker programming and allows much more flexible modifications to be carried out. Standard applications include payments, communication, logistics and order processing. It resembles Lego in a way, whereby each block is a microservice. By combining blocks, completely different structures (applications) can be made.

A microservice architecture involves the application being split up into a number of small components, the microservices. This is in contrast to the classic method of system development (monolithic), which was based on an integrated program (software application). This application runs independently and is not coupled, which means that any modifications have to be carried out in each monolithic system. At the heart of microservices, however, is the coupling between other systems via application program interfaces (APIs) and one's own logarithms that consist of coupled microservices. Figure 2 shows the difference between the integral approach of monolithic systems and the coupled approach of microservices. For the competitive strength in dynamic markets it is speed of action that is essential, which is why so many companies choose to use microservices these days. If, however, traditional organisations still continue to use the monolithic systems, they will quickly fall behind the competition due to their sluggish ability to change.

> The debate between monolithic architectures, wherein centralization takes precedence, versus microservice construction, which holds that specialized and insular tasks are best left to themselves, has entered a new era with Docker[3] and its ilk. But it's more than architecture, it's a culture of thought.[4]

Due to the many new techniques based on open source coding (such as Docker), the differences between speed of modification, and sharing of

---

[3] Docker is a computer program that performs operating-system-level virtualisation, also known as 'containerization'. It was first released in 2013 and was developed by Docker, Inc. Docker is used to run software packages called 'containers'. *Source*: Wikipedia.

[4] *Source:* https://dzone.com/articles/monolithic-vs-microservice-architecture.

Monolithic approach   Microservices approach/architecture

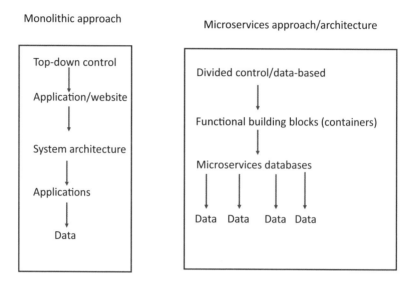

Figure 2.   The difference between the integral approach of monolithic systems and the coupled approach of microservices.

functions and information are becoming increasingly important. The above quote illustrates this clearly. There is a change currently underway between the central systems (monolithic) and the flexible approach such as microsystems. The new techniques that are based on a container approach are also in line with this change. With microservices this concerns small programs aimed at functions that are coupled in algorithms. With containers, the application has been made more stable, but still retains flexibility. In a container, all the relevant programmes are coupled at function level after which the functions are in turn coupled to one another through the containers (Figure 3). The principle is the same as with microservices, which is why it is worth noting that it is no longer just the architecture alone, but also the philosophy that determines the competitive strength. By applying new technologies quickly and responding immediately to changes in the behaviour of customers and businesses, as platform companies and start-ups do, companies will be able to grow quickly. This allows them to quickly attack traditional organisations. These traditional organisations will be attacked evermore frequently by new entrants with a new (system) philosophy.

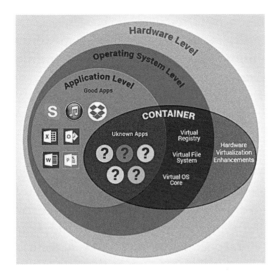

Figure 3.   The application of containers as part of a system.

Application Containerisation versus Virtualisation and System Containers

All information and relevant systems can be coupled to one another by means of a container. These containers support a particular system function in all facets. By coupling containers, a flexible system is created.

Server virtualisation abstracts the operating system and the application from the underlying hardware or virtual sources. A hypervisor layer[5] is located between the memory, computer usage and storage on the one hand and the operating system, application and services on the other. A container is a standard unit of software that packages up code and all its dependencies, so that the application runs quickly and reliably from one computer environment to another. A container in fact contains all relevant software and data that is necessary for a particular application. It uses the traditional data and systems as can be seen in Figure 3. This form of pro-

---

[5]A hypervisor or virtual machine monitor (VMM) is a computer software, firmware or hardware that creates and runs virtual machines. A computer on which a hypervisor runs one or more virtual machines is called a host machine, and each virtual machine is called a guest machine. *Source*: Wikipedia.

gramming enables a rapid response to changes in the technology and applications, while still allowing standard programs on components to be used. The container is in fact the specific market-oriented application that uses traditional core systems and data.

What is the Competitive Strength Offered by IT?

The speed at which systems can be modified (in terms of technology and the organisation) determines the competitive strength of organisations in dynamic markets. This is why an SOA should form the basis. This provides direct insight into the relationship between customers and supplier, and allows for a direct response to a supplier's wishes (often product and service oriented) as well as to the wishes of customers, often purchase oriented. This application within microservices and possibly a container helps to create great flexibility and a clear focus on the wishes, the customer-based supply. The basic principles of an SOA lead to links to other systems whereby APIs are used. The API specifies the link of both the sender and receiver. The use of APIs results in a great deal of flexibility, and allows for systems and applications to be coupled to one another at function or data level without this being visible for the user.

The use of cloud computing is another system element that is important for the new system set-up, and consequently for the competitive strength. Cloud computing allows applications to be connected, which can be accessed anywhere. The system elements ensure that an organisation is no longer an independent entity with its own systems, but part of a greater network system. This is also the condition for creating the previously mentioned network effects. This stratification of the system application and the management of this within a dynamic environment require specific systems. The decision also has to be made regarding what an organisation has to do itself and what can be outsourced. Whatever the decision, however, the focus has to remain on the behaviour and wishes of customers (business-to-consumer (B2C) and business-to-business (B2B)) and the required competitive strength. The core of the system will have to facilitate this through, for example, a microservice environment with independent program blocks as described previously. This enables a competitive

Device level: mobile, sensors, computers	Top layer, used in sectors and products.
Business activity level, interaction, connectivity	Use in application areas and channels (the Internet) as well as devices such as sensors, mobile phone, cameras.
Applications including search, algorithms and AI	Applications: Layer including speech, text, chat and services related to content.
Data, logics and business rules, access protection	Core of the system: internet and interfaces to external systems. The system is entirely set up according to the relationship with the market and customers in a dynamic market.
Databases, external connections, cloud access 3rd party access	

Figure 4.   Application of cloud computing in organisations.

advantage to be achieved through closer customer relationships and innovation. This can also be embedded within the organisation's business model and revenue model (Figure 4).

What are the Strategic Choices of an Organisation?

For organisations it is a challenge to change from a traditional organisation, with a linear approach (supply chain), to an organisation focused on collaboration and the wishes of the customer. For the systems this means a change: from systems that support the traditional business process to systems that guide the relationship with the customers and the market. This change in system (and strategy) is fundamental for success. An organisation must be fully aware of this, and should also ask itself whether this strategic change away from the traditional business systems, such as ERP or customer relationship management (CRM), is possible or whether modifications have to be made, or perhaps an entirely new system is needed. A decision not so much about systems but, rather, a new strategy, a new business model, and more specific organisation form. Systems provide support.

The traditional organisation is based on traditional market relationships and traditional competitive relationships. There is generally a hierarchical decision-making structure. The structure is aimed at control and top-down communication and management. If, however, the customer is taken as the starting point, a different sort of control is necessary, namely one based on customer and market contacts. The market or product suddenly no longer guides the process (marketing is 'to market'), but the wishes and the behaviour of customers do. This requires a flat organisation with an integrated provision of information and central decision-making. The organisation will usually change from a hierarchical organisation to a much flatter function-based organisation focused on added value. Moreover, there is also the culture within an organisation. It is difficult, perhaps even impossible, to change an organisation's culture. The culture is embedded within the behaviour of the people, the traditional processes and the traditional control and management methods, not to mention the structure of the entire organisation. It is practically impossible to turn a traditional organisation into a platform-based organisation. **The organisations are strongly sales-oriented (supply-oriented), in which the systems have a subordinate role. Systems hereby lead to greater efficiency in and insight into the processes. The systems are seldom externally-oriented, with a focus on competitive strength and value creation.** However, it is of course possible to start a separate unit or start-up business based on the new strategy (customer demand-driven) and new technology. Such a change would require a radical decision with plenty of uncertainty, but with a significant impact on the market if applied successfully.

> Spotify, as a platform, operates a freemium business model (basic services are free, whilst additional functions are offered through a paid subscription). Spotify receives the content of major record labels and independent artists, and pays royalties on the streamed music.

Do Squads Lead to Innovation?

Another possibility is the formation of squads. Within the organisation a small group works on innovation projects. This group is not connected with a particular department or function, but has been put together from various disciplines. The group works independently, but provides periodic feedback to discuss and report on the progress. Google, for example, has hundreds of these 'informal' teams working on innovative applications, sometimes alongside one another on the same innovation. They are allowed to spend one day a week on a project. As soon as the group has a concrete plan or product, they present this to a larger group of staff members. Here they try to win support to further develop their idea. In the past, 3M employed the same innovative stimulus. This is how post-its came about. A member of staff wondered what he could do with a glue product that was to be disposed of as the adhesive quality was not so good. In a small team, a squad, they went looking for a solution until they discovered the now well-known application. And so a multimillion-dollar product was born.

Google has put together its squads from a small group of developers and one product owner, usually, but not necessarily, a product manager. What makes the squad unique?

- First of all, the teams are responsible for the functional areas of the company's product line; they do not work on entire products or on *ad hoc* projects that are assigned by the management. A team may, for example, concentrate solely on search technology. As a result, the company is able to develop considerable expertise and intellectual capital for every functional area of its products and services. In other words, it can develop teams of true industry experts instead of a single large team of coding generalists.
- The second way in which they differ from the traditional organisation approaches is that they get real autonomy. In actual fact, Google regards it squads as independent start-ups.

What does this mean in practical terms? This means that a squad can select its own areas of functional responsibility in which it wishes to work. As soon as the team has taken over such an area, the product's production version can be modified at any given moment. It can train users without having to wait for the approval of someone outside the team.

The basic idea is that squads can lead to a much more efficient product development, as well as to teams that are well informed about the various functional areas of the product, have faster development cycles and ultimately develop more successful products. But is this approach suitable for every organisation? Well, that depends. There are both advantages and disadvantages, and it clearly does not suit every organisational culture. It requires a flexible and open organisation with a limited hierarchy. An open communication structure and a sense of community are also important.

Many organisations are either unable or unwilling to undergo such a change. The decision can then be made to outsource the customer approach and the resulting change. In doing so, the companies join other providers, at product level. The previously mentioned aggregators, the sales platforms (single-sided) provide the opportunity here as host. By using these platforms, a new distribution channel is created alongside the existing traditional distribution channels such as shops, distributors and the like. This requires no major modifications to the traditional organisation and traditional systems. The traditional business model can remain intact. A greater dependency on these sales platforms, however, will arise, as there is no disruption or innovation. The competitive strength will also decrease, as you would be dependent upon an aggregator, pay commission for this and be part of an overall supply of similar products on the sales platform. The focus would remain on products, the offer and transactions (Figure 5).

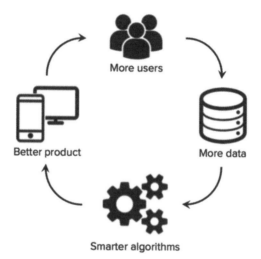

Figure 5.   Strategy formulation and competitive strength is based on customer behaviour which requires constant and sequential analyses.

The possibilities offered by technology and expectations of customers change quickly. Companies therefore have to be constantly aware of these changes and be able to identify them in order to stay relevant. In addition to analysis systems, data mining systems can also be installed in order to monitor social media and classify and analyse Internet searches (for example, through Google Analytics along with specific analysis tools), to clarify what customers want and how they want it.

Will the Supply Chain Implode?

Forbes technology executives suggest that observing sector events (for example, trade fairs and newsletters) and news collection websites are easy and accurate ways of identifying the changes, both current and potential. In this way, it is simple for managers to follow all the developments and become truly inspired to innovate and think about how opportunities can be exploited for the core of the value proposition. Nobody really knows, however, what the future will bring and what the impact of technology will be on companies and networks in general.

Constant modification of products and services and the emergence of new providers result in increasingly more new products entering the market that are different, more advanced and often also cheaper. In order to offer some resistance to this, it is necessary to have a strong focus on the behaviour of the customers as well as constantly monitor market developments. This is identified and analysed through a platform. This process is difficult if it is not automated. Studies are too *ad hoc*, often subjective and pose questions from the perspective of the provider (such as: Are you satisfied?). The value of the analyses of the customer behaviour is then not objective enough to base a decision on or to identify changes; the identification of alternatives, the (dormant) wishes and the potential network effects for decision-making.

A number of components are important for supporting the buying behaviour, such as follows:

- What are the customer wishes?
- What are the best products for meeting those wishes?

- How can services contribute to a complete supply?
- How can analyses of visitors and historic search and buying behaviour contribute to a good match?

This requires a matching module for, which includes the following:

- the match of product or service solutions to customers' needs;
- a link with relevant service products and external providers;
- a supplier-independent search process;
- achieving exponential growth through external links and by facilitating needs-driven demand.

In fact, a platform becomes a paradigm, a reflection of reality. The platform attracts visitors, and the visitors in turn specify a need. The translation is made to the matching module, whereby a needs-based solution (products or services) is offered. And then a sale can take place. The platform facilitates all the steps in the process (Figure 6).

A distinction can be made between these multisided platforms and generic platforms. Nowadays everything that has any form of visible collaboration is called a platform. However, these are usually portals,

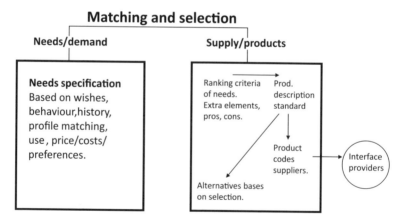

Figure 6.   The matching process on a platform.

or aggregation platforms that are not disruptive. These platforms offer a third party the possibility of offering products through sales-oriented 'platforms' (aggregators), for example, Bol.com, Coolblue or other sales-oriented applications. The strength lies in the possibility for other providers (also small ones) to take advantage of the appeal of these providers. They pay a commission for this, which is sometimes as high as 20% of the sales price. This is actually nothing new. It is a classic sales model that we have already seen in the *shop in shop* system and consignments. The owner of the platform benefits the most from this; a bigger product range without additional costs, but with extra revenue. It is also a sign of the powerlessness of traditional parties who join such providers that are in fact their competitors. The provider can see straightaway how much you sell, what your revenues are and which customers find your products interesting. This is all information that is of use to the provider who will use it to improve his strategy. Selling the articles through such a platform only really makes sense if you are not able to develop a strong online strategy of your own (too few visitors). Such a platform boosts the online sales, but costs around 10% to 20% of the turnover. Such a choice may offer a short-term solution, but is seldom viable in the long term (too low revenues).

Automating Platforms

When automating platforms on the basis of networks a number of aspects are important. As people log in from various locations, and a wide range of suppliers are involved, the system is facilitated in the cloud. Market leaders here are Amazon Web Services (AWS), Microsoft's Azure and Google Cloud. According to Forrester, these market leaders have acquired an almost unassailable position. What is more, a distinction has to be made between the front end, which facilitates the contacts through an excellent user experience, manages the logic and takes care of the matching. And on the other hand, the back-end, the core of the system. This core element takes care of the administrative functions, the monitoring, the analyses, the process control and connecting the various external systems. This back-end includes, for example, the interfaces to external parties such

A possible solution with standard components

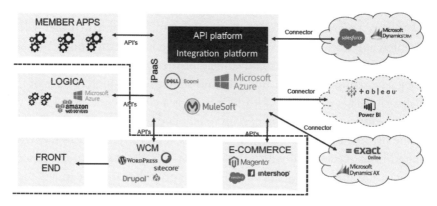

Figure 7.   Technical concept of system connections.

Source: Datacon, Tilburg.

as the suppliers (at product level), the service providers, the advertisers and the independent applications.

And *another criterium* is the necessary flexibility. Speedy adaptation is needed if there are changes in the market, if new providers emerge or if the customer behaviour changes (for example, through network effects). The purpose of the platform is to facilitate in the buying process of products and services for both standard products and custom-made products (such as with concepts, tendering, services and specific products) (Figure 7).

An appropriate way of realising this is to first make an analysis of the following required functions of a platform:

- required functions;
- user stories;
- translation into objects;
- specification of processes;
- making a high-level design;
- an implementation based on agile concepts (such as SCRUM, Kanban). During this implementation the final functionality and priority are determined.

Based on the model illustrated in Figure 5, the following specific functions can be identified:

- **Platform orchestration:** This describes the operation of a platform, from logging in to carrying out the activities. It includes the login procedure, the matching, a language functionality, the links to other systems, a process description per component, order registration and various management functions such as administration communication. These are front end functions.
- **Analytics:** The analysis of the behaviour on the platform: searching, looking and matching. This forms the basis for the analyses. It results in data ponds, big data, which tell much more about the buying behaviour and form the basis for more knowledge and direct communication. This is the link to an external system.
- **API:** APIs are the interface programs that connect a component of the platform (such as product choice or information) with an external provider. This may not only be a product provider but also an external system such as CRM, analyses and ERP. This is a core component of the platform.
- **Member apps:** Through this authorisation the visitor has access to the site. An authorisation can be a simple detail such as customer number, email address and postcode/house number, or a more complex authorisation whereby certain details are necessary which first have to be verified before an access code can be issued. External databases, such as the database of the Chamber of Commerce, can also function as a means of verification and authorisation.
- **Authentication:** This is a process for checking whether a user, another computer or application is actually what they claim to be. The authentication verifies whether a given proof of identity corresponds with security/authentication features, for example, some form of proof registered in the system. Passwords and verification questions are also possible.
- **The product function, services and clustering:** This includes the product and service description, whereby, along with the product features, the user needs are specified as well. This also involves the classification of these user needs. Customers specify their wishes, after which the matching takes place with products and services with the same features (Figure 8).

Customer wishes/needs product specification

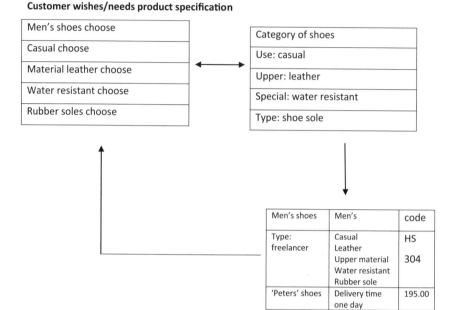

Figure 8.   Filtering example.

The product file is a database with all products, irrespective of suppliers. It is only once a selection is made that the supplier is mentioned with the product. Of course, if a search is carried out on the basis of supplier alone, then the supplier will be shown together with general criteria from the supplier database. This uncoupling of supplier and products allows matches to be carried out on the basis of need and product. In older applications you first had to look for a supplier, after which this supplier was linked to a supplier's website; the affiliate model as described earlier.

The matching lies at the heart of a multisided platform; matching between individual needs and products. In addition, there is the link to suppliers. The platform is an intermediary that connects all the services necessary for the purchase and use of the products and services (Figure 9).

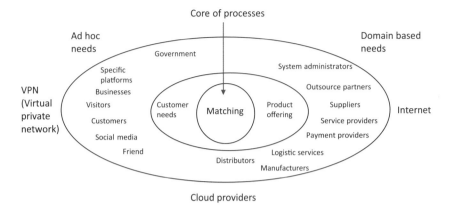

Figure 9.   Model of a multisided platform based on the mediation function. The core is mediation (matching). The supporting functions are shown in the outer section and can be subdivided into front end, back-end and external.

How do Organisations and the Relationships Change as a Result of Technology?

Technology can be applied in various ways: for efficiency, quality improvement and for collaboration. Particularly this latter application leads to disruption. This is in part because structures change; however, the relationship with customers change as well. The technological application results in more knowledge of the customer, enabling companies to respond more effectively to their customers' needs and wishes. The direct relationships between producers and customers can also form the basis of change. Wholesalers have to redefine their role, and so do the shops. The availability of products is no longer what sets them apart, but rather the knowledge of both customer wishes and the products that can satisfy these wishes. It is no longer relevant to think in terms of transactions, but in relationships. Organisations have to respond to the rapid (technical) changes and be flexible. New automation techniques such as microservices ensure for a flexible automation application. Organisations should no longer work in a hierarchical manner, but offer space for flexibility and innovation. Squads are one way of realising this.

Chapter 7

It is about Customers, Not Products: A Change of Vision

In the supply economy, it is all about selling more. Marketing was used to bring about transactions. There was a competition between providers vying for the attention of customers. Market positions, market shares, sales, profit margins and the distribution channel were important indicators. The customer is the endpoint in the supply economy, as can be seen in the various *customer journeys*. At the very most, some aftercare is given after the purchase, but this is often regarded merely as an expense. This can be seen in the lack of a contact button on websites, the long queues on the telephone and the lengthy wait for an answer to an email (and sometimes no response at all). Sometimes, this aftercare, the customer contact centre, is outsourced to a third party, which invoices the company for the costs made, such as the number of calls and the duration of the calls. Efficiency is the aim, not the quality of the answer or support. Sometimes, there is no strategy involved in this at all (or this has to be paid for). This approach centres upon a constant battle for the buyer, despite years of evidence showing that it is much cheaper to retain a customer than to find a new one. However, this does not fit in with the supply model and the marketing. Marketing is regarded as a support function that costs a great deal of money. In times of declining profits, companies often look for cost savings in the marketing department, while a countercyclical approach would be better. If sales decrease, it is important that companies focus more on their existing customers. Competition increasingly will shift to one based on the loyalty and strength of one's customer base. The approach, based on the supply economy, is a short-term strategy whereby companies seek to set themselves apart from the competition. The purpose of marketing can be defined as: creating, communicating and delivering 'value' to a target group (Fahy and Jobber, 2015).

How has Marketing Changed?

In the course of the years the purpose of marketing has not changed; the principles and processes, however, have. Marketing has changed in order to be able to respond quickly to the rapid changes and dynamics of the modern market conditions. The increase of data, based on users and network-based business models, has made marketing decisions more customised and specialised. Classic marketing was all about the supply, while future developments are demand based. It is difficult to be distinctive in terms of product; it is more and more about the value exchange. The consumer is looking for something, the supplier offers it; the distinction lies in the customer contacts, the service and the targeted communication at an individual level. The supply provides the solution for a need (Figure 1).

Back in 2000 already, Dolan[1] had argued for a reorientation of marketing, for a shift from product- and supply-oriented marketing, to marketing aimed at creating value. Three steps were suggested for this: first segmentation of the market, then selecting the target group and finally optimally positioning the product or service among the potential buyers. A customer has a set of buying criteria, which are important for the choice. It is this set of criteria that plays an important role in the modern buying behaviour via the filters of a platform. The degree to which the provider responds to the individual wishes, based on the detected personal preferences, determines to a large degree the value of the supply. In addition to this value creation, knowledge of the individual wishes is important. In the

---

[1] Dolan, Robert J. (1997). Note on Marketing Strategy, *Harvard Business Review*, revised in 2000.

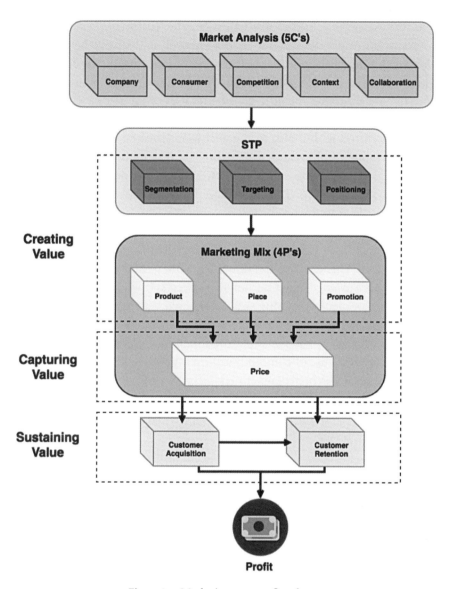

Figure 1.   Marketing strategy flowchart.

past, the classic marketing mix and marketing instruments were used. Due to the application of technology, this has now become much simpler.

A forgotten element in the classic marketing approach is investigating what a customer is willing to pay. This *willingness to pay* (WTP) is strongly determined by the value proposition. Why is the customer prepared to pay more for an Apple smartphone than a Huawei? A strong element here is the positioning of the product in the mind of the consumer (perception). Other values include design, availability, experience and references. On the Internet, the customer is able to get a better idea of the values, which influences his WTP a particular price. This value determination applies not only to the product but also to the decision regarding where to buy that product: online, offline and which shop or distributor. The traditional competition between price providers and service providers (such as shops) is a consequence of this. This is not about price, but about the value that customers attach to the product. Price, however, can be an element; mind you, if it were the only element, then only the cheaper providers would survive, which is not the case. The term *commodification* has been mentioned before. This refers to the value, also with a transaction, being more than just an *exchange* based on tangible aspects. It is precisely due to the recent developments that this should be used as a control element for marketing. On the Internet, buying is easy and convenient and has many other advantages, but it remains functional. Niche players and physical contacts can make use of commodification aspects such as service, perception, advice and personal contact making a customer willing to pay more. If a customer chooses only functional sales via the Internet, an almost impossible competition arises for niche providers and physical contact points (as can be seen with Aliexpress).

The Choice of Distribution Channel

The provider's choice of distribution channel rested upon three selection criteria:

- Location: A location close to the 'market' was essential, not only for business-to-business (B2B) sales, which required staff and production means, but also for business-to-consumer (B2C). Due to the limited mobility of buyers, companies carried out their marketing on a local level. Classic marketing was based on a clear, linear distribution method (linear supply chain).

- Based on the approach of target groups: Via sellers, agents and trade-shows, links in the supply chain were approached or sellers were approached directly (particularly in B2B). This direct approach was also employed as a distribution channel for direct sales such as with mail-order companies (*direct sales* channel).
- Intensity of the channel whereby customer wishes are the priority: With the Internet, there is often a hybrid channel or it is a combination of methods and possibilities — direct sales and sales via shops, communication via the Internet, a different method of sales, or an integration of the possibilities.

In classic marketing, the choice of distribution channel plays an important role. Traditionally, this was the chosen physical distribution channel, whereby reliability, reach, image and pricing were important elements for reaching the intended target group. (1) In the early 1990s, we saw some change in this due to the growth of mail-order companies and direct marketing. Here, a virtual channel was developed alongside the physical one. This resulted in a split in how the market was approached: B2B used sellers, but agents and sellers were also important in other markets for stimulating sales. In the new direct marketing approach, however, the purchasers determined which articles were sold. It became increasingly important to have a direct channel available via direct mail, telemarketing and direct selling in new ways (in television programmes and later through the Internet). (2) As manufacturers wanted to approach the entire market, a coordinated approach emerged between the channels with their own dynamics. The channel choice became ever more expedient: How can the target group best be approached, in a mass market and with small specific target groups? It became possible to use various channels in addition to a selective distribution.

Furthermore, it became necessary to have information about customers and the market. It was simpler to gain this information through a direct sale and when using CRM methods (methods whereby customer data form the basis for communication).

A final consideration (3) was the intensity of the channel. What is the expectation of the target group and what is the association with the distribution point, physical or direct?

As customers were given a choice between the growing direct marketing market (and the emergence of Internet sales) and the physical locations, the preference of a customer also became important. Were customers prepared to travel, whether a short or long distance, to a distribution point such as a shop? What price was acceptable considering the higher costs of a distribution point? Were customers willing to pay extra to pick up the articles from the shop themselves, or visit a distribution point like a showroom? And finally: What costs and efforts were necessary on the part of the manufacturer and the distribution point to motivate customers?

In the last few decades, it has become increasingly clear that customers had a growing preference for the new possibilities of direct buying/sales over sales through a physical distribution point. This led to an increasing tension between the manufacturers and the classic distribution points (such as shops) and between the physical distribution points and webshops. This conflict came about as a result of the following:

- the manufacturers' wish to sell the products at every distribution point (online or offline) desired by the customer;
- the limited capacity of distribution points to adapt (clinging onto old values);
- not being able to adequately translate the higher costs of a distribution point to values for a customer (commodification).

In all the activities between the various parties, it is the customer who guides the buying process. The customer chooses which channel and which values are important in the purchase. The challenge for manufacturers and distribution points is to respond to this with the right value creation and value exchange. The price is considered as a means of communication.

The price is a unit comprising product-based costs, service, quality, image and perception. This total value is expressed in the price. A lower price would require a compromise on one of the elements such as service, availability or quality. This can be seen with, for example, many Chinese products, where the adage 80% quality for 60% of the price applies. Buying products and services therefore involves an exchange of value.

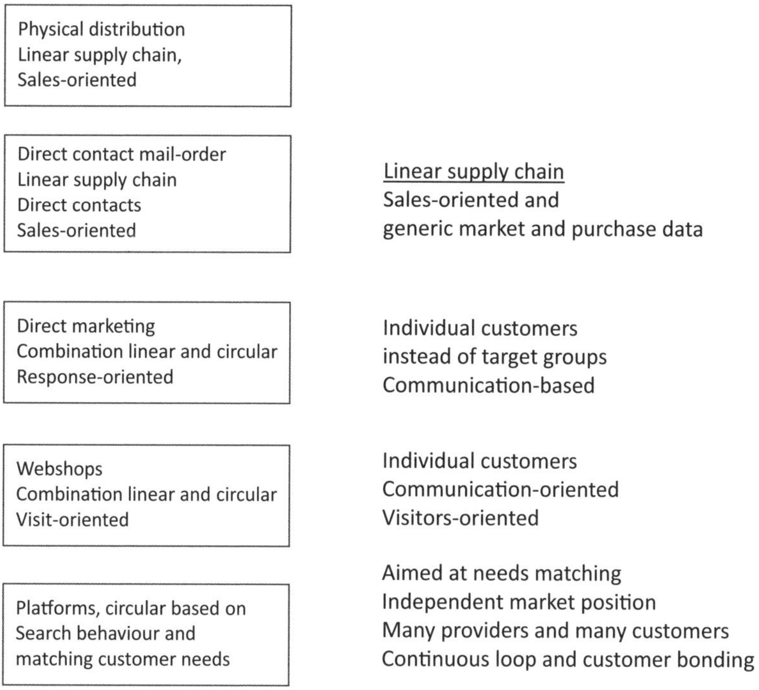

Physical distribution
Linear supply chain,
Sales-oriented

Direct contact mail-order
Linear supply chain
Direct contacts
Sales-oriented

Linear supply chain
Sales-oriented and
generic market and purchase data

Direct marketing
Combination linear and circular
Response-oriented

Individual customers
instead of target groups
Communication-based

Webshops
Combination linear and circular
Visit-oriented

Individual customers
Communication-oriented
Visitors-oriented

Platforms, circular based on
Search behaviour and
matching customer needs

Aimed at needs matching
Independent market position
Many providers and many customers
Continuous loop and customer bonding

Figure 2. Development of supply chains (supply-oriented) to platforms (needs-oriented).

The traditional development from direct marketing, via webshops, to multisided platforms is an example of a development with a different value creation. The flexibility of the traditional entrants was perfect for responding to customer preferences. This does not involve a short-term position; through analyses and modifications, platforms will aim for a long-term value creation with associated customer bonding (the customer loop and algorithms support this, Figure 2).

Traditional competition focuses on the value sustainability. How can you maintain the value during the purchasing relative to the competition as well as during the buying process? This is no longer possible on the basis of classic instruments and a classic market-oriented strategy. Old marketing activities lose impact as they are supply driven (usually a comparative competitive advantage). The old strategy revolved around having a better proposition than the competitions. The future focus is on bonding customers through a positive value exchange. It is therefore no longer a matter of a comparison with the competitors, but one of a solid bond with customers. Costs and the old selection criteria and buying locations are losing value. Value has to be created for the customer in some other way. Technology plays a dominant, if not all-encompassing, role in this.

The role that technology plays is based on the efficiency of traditional processes. Technology lies at the heart of the change when adapting processes to the customers' extent of technology adoption (Figure 3).

The technology plays a leading role in the change only once customers apply as well as accept it. This applies particularly in the buying process during which value creation and value sustainability are important (Tables 1 and 2).

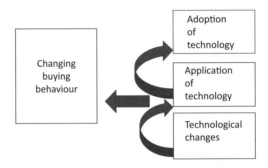

Figure 3.   Dominant role of technology in change of buying behaviour.

Table 1.   Classic marketing versus platform marketing.

	Traditional Marketing	Platform Marketing
Strategy focus	Pushing strategy	Pulling strategy customers
	Porter's generic strategy	Interaction at any moment
	Value sustainability	
Methodology	Marketing mix	Marketing mix
	Mass marketing	Customised marketing
		Multisided value creation
Instruments	Multichannel 4P's	Network effects
		Viral Strategy
		Big data

Table 2.   Overview of changes and adapted focus.

Tactic	Shift	New Focus
Article	Changing customer needs brings about a change with the demand for (perception) custom-made products.	Active collaboration with partners to provide everyone with an individualised product experience.
Promotion	Consumers no longer need the provider for more information, but want interaction with the company or other customers for specific questions.	No longer sending general information to customers, whether online or offline, but rather responding actively to questions. Customers are not so much concerned with information, but rather with involvement/engagement.
Price	The prices are no longer set in stone (permanent), but have become dynamic, often individually determined per channel or per customer.	Active monitoring of the prices of competitors and trying to adapt quickly. Personal prices help to create a bond with customers.
Place	Purchases can be made anywhere due to the application of the Internet.	Allowing customers to participate in all channels, the same experience with all touchpoints.
People	The focus on customers requires specific skills. IT is becoming increasingly dominant, but new (IT) skills are required.	Recruiting people with the right skills. The right skills are necessary in order to monitor consumers and competitors.
Processes	Changing needs of the consumer bring about a necessity to modify products/services, which is not possible with the linear supply chains.	Companies have to move away from the linear supply chain, which is not able to match good solutions with the needs of the modern customer, who has an individual need. Collaboration as well as sharing processes and information with expert partners is necessary. Supporting individual search behaviour.
Productivity and quality	Added values were never as important as they are now. Consumer bonds are created, and these consumers buy only if you have added value that will motivate them.	Constantly assessing the added value in the 'value proposition' and actively measuring whether this is still of value. If this is not the case, customers will leave.
Physical environment	Services and experiences are new drives in the market, integral with online possibilities and smartphones.	Ensure that the value proposition, both online and offline, can be communicated at every touchpoint. Experience and communication are decisive factors in the traditional market. Ensure therefore that you can offer your customers a good experience and provide them the possibility of communicating about this with one another (for example, via social media, *customer reviews*).

The change of focus involves a focus on continuous relationships, and on offering additional value before, during and after the purchase. It is all about creating bonds and meeting the individual wishes of the customers. In the old model, there is a temporary bond based on the product and distribution point. Each time, the customer has to be motivated to buy all over again. Mass media was the right tool in the mid-1980s, which was then followed by direct marketing in the 1990s. These days, these are only components of 'promotion'. The bond consists more of the following:

- identification with the brand/product;
- loyalty towards a distribution point due to location, service and involvement (hedonistic factors);
- direct communication, remote and real time;
- personal service.

Due to the customers' wish for a stronger bond and more convenience, choices will increasingly be made out of habit. In the physical model, people used to buy from the same shop because it was nearby. These days, due to the Internet and increased mobility, people can buy anywhere. The shop has to prove its added value all over again. Customers will occasionally also buy from other providers. Emotional purchases may be made in a shopping centre or on the high street. Rational purchases on the other hand are made locally or at smaller providers that can offer extra services. Customers no longer being loyal to just a single provider is referred to as *multihoming*. They buy from a range of identical shops for well-considered reasons (based on identified values). Customers are committed to more than one option; they buy just as easily online from Bol.com, as they do from a local shop. This pattern is reinforced by the Internet, which makes every competitor a mere click away (Figure 4).

How can You Still Compete?

Through multihoming, there is increasing pressure on the bonding of customers, the return behaviour. In Chapter 6, the RFM analysis was described as a dynamic means of analysis for determining the bonding factor: at a particular moment and in succession. This provides a good

Figure 4.   The loyalty loop model (Edelman and Singer, 2015).

indication of the multihoming of customers and can be done at buying level, as well as search and social media levels. Purchases are made at more than one shop. People search for goods on Google, but also increasingly search on websites of popular providers such as Coolblue, Amazon, Airbnb or Bol.com. The websites of these providers are used instead of the Google Search function. Multihoming is also part of the platform strategy, as a platform offers a product range from many suppliers. Multihoming has become embedded in the *single homing* strategy of platforms. Platforms employ a *single homing* strategy. Bonding customers, creating loyalty and ensuring return behaviour.

In the classic approach, the reason to buy was stable; the added value for the customer did not actually change and the number of entrants in the market was limited (see Porter's Five Forces Model). Due to the wide range of products and services offered on the Internet, the choice is practically unlimited, but it therefore also lacks transparency. This is one reason that there is such tough competition on the Internet. In order to provide customers with a better overview of the market and to be able to take advantage of the added value provided by the Internet, there is a consolidation of the supply. This consolidation is not only based on supply, such as via portals and aggregators, but also via the platforms.

Each platform has a particular value proposition from which the customer can choose. A sales platform (aggregator) such as Alibaba, a platform that supports the purchase (based on the customer journey) such as JD.com, and a selection platform (P2P) such as Airbnb and Uber. Each platform has clear distinctive values that are communicated to the customer.

The change in strategy of MediaMarkt in 2018 (metro) can be seen in this context. The value proposition, which consisted of the shops' long opening hours and a low price image, was no longer distinctive enough. Particularly, the success of electronic webshops helped to encourage the company to focus more on the customer and in particular to support the information process (pre-purchase). Once a customer has decided on a product, the delivery also has to meet the expectations (the same experience with every *touchpoint*), while during this process there also has to be constant communication in order to maintain the relationship. What is more, a focus based on transaction margin is difficult if other parties offer more value and stipulate a better price for this, or if there are other revenue models possible other than ones based on transaction profits.

The customer experiences can be measured using an experience study based on the *net promoter* score. This net promoter score allows customers to rate the services. This forms part of the strategy and any necessary modifications of the concept. Within the concept used by smaller webshops, the pre-sales phase is important. Support using independent product information, such as videos, chatting and of course the telephone helpline are media that support this. In addition, within Hybrid concepts (multichannel), there is a physical channel where customers receive support when buying a product. This advice channel is an addition to the online channel (and not the other way round). The purpose is to provide advice and support in the purchase. The number of products stocked by such a shop is very limited, but the orders can be placed online directly. This shop is usually not in a shopping area, but on the outskirts of a city, where there are good accessibility and parking facilities. There is currently a total of seven shops that support the buying process.

> What all this means to managers is that they must pay attention to how their companies create experience value in both the physical world and the virtual world, separately or in combination. To create a superior service experience in the new realm of activity, executives must understand the differences between value creation in the offline marketplace and the online marketspace. Service companies can not only create value through the online service platform, but also extract value from such platforms by organizing and synthesizing the information generated by customer usage of self-service technologies.

Moreover, opening the marketspace to bring additional actors into the service platform — and thereby providing multiple new value propositions — is beneficial to customers. However, managers need to evaluate the potential benefits and risks of opening resources when multiple actors become involved in activities to create experiential value. The marketspace could provide opportunities to more actors, and they should mainly focus on certain points of activity during the transport service process, because the information in the marketspace can be a potential source of new revenue.[2]

The Customer Experience Process

The customer experience process has three stages and flows from pre-purchase to purchase to post purchase. The process is dynamic and iterative (Lemon and Verhoef, 2016). Customers experience touch points in each stage (Lemon and Verhoef, 2016). So, the customer experience can be conceptualized, as shown in Figure 5.

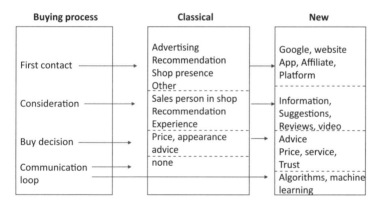

Figure 5.   From customer journey to customer engagement to customer interaction.

---

[2] *Source*: Chaoren Lu, Wei Geng, and Iris Wang (2015). The Role of Self-Service Mobile Technologies in the Creation of Customer Travel Experiences, *Technology Innovation Management Review*, February 2015.

Bibliography

Edelman, D. C. and Singer, M. (2015). Competing on customer journeys, *Harvard Business Review*, November 2015.

Fahy J. and Jobber, D. (2015). *Foundations of Marketing*, Mc Graw-Hill.

Lemon, K. N. and Verhoef, P. C. (2016). Understanding customer experience throughout the customer journey, *Journal of Marketing*, November 2016. doi: https://doi.org/10.1509/jm.15.0420

Chapter 8

New Marketing and Competition Principles through the Adoption of Technology

As described in the previous chapters, technology has been responsible not only for a change in the buying behaviour of customers but also in the products and services offered by suppliers. This change took place in parallel with companies in the business-to-business (B2B) market and in the consumer market. In certain market situations, it was the linking of systems and the collaboration in, for example, the cloud that were important. In the consumer market, however, the change very much lay in the acceptance of a new buying channel, the adoption of the smartphone by consumers and the change in the buying behaviour due to socio-economic circumstances.

For the consumer market, this led to a shift from a supply-driven approach to a demand-driven approach. The consumer market fragmented into individuals, forming target groups of varying compositions — similar to atoms, in a way, which form various connections with other atoms to create different substances at a molecular level (comparable with the target groups), or in marketing terms: display a different behaviour.

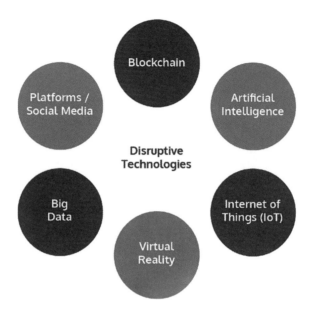

Figure 1. Disruptive technologies.

The challenge lies not only in recognising this different behaviour but also in identifying the components that lead to this behaviour; just as it is important for physicists to be able to break down the individual molecules into atoms. This is not an easy process, as it requires different specialisations and different tools. The new technologies offer these tools in the form of big data analyses (Figure 1). By analysing every aspect of data, as well as examining the links and the connections of the data elements, one can gain knowledge about the buying behaviour, and ascribe predictive values to this. This knowledge is an important source for the competition strategy. If this knowledge is insufficient, or even lacking, any competitors who do possess this knowledge will have a major advantage. Just consider, for example, the lack of this knowledge among shops, while the large Internet providers have this information. The adoption of technology by companies in the consumer market has led to an adaptation of the strategy and development of new distribution channels and methods. Knowledge of the customers' buying motives gave rise to a disruption in markets (Figure 2).

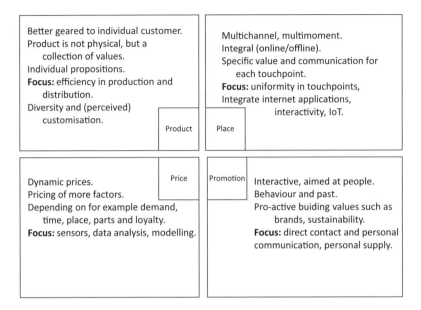

Figure 2.   Disruption on the basis of classic marketing instruments.

B2B, from Efficiency to Disruption

A similar transition is taking place in the B2B market. Here, the focus on the distribution channel is of particular importance. As long as the business connections are based on a complex of buying motives, the old values remain important. These include the regular contacts, the delivery times, the collaboration between the various links in the supply chain and the dependency upon one another. There is a strong costs and price focus alongside clear agreements regarding delivery, production and quality. Personal contacts not only ensure bonding but are also required for necessary information, upstream and downstream. Trade fairs, personal visits and other touchpoints are also important.

Due to the limited market size, there is transparency in the market. The parties look closely at one another from the perspective of the supply. The application of the technology has also changed this market. At first, the cost/price factor was important. Efficiency was important not only for a different price level but also for better connections. Electronic data interchange (EDI) led to efficiency, as well as to a closer connection between parties (on product basis). Most B2B markets are conservative, with a hierarchical organisation for efficiency and control. And this is why these organisations respond slowly to changes in the market. The culture is also conservative, resulting in the people who work in the organisation also being conservative (after all, companies tend to look for people that fit both the job requirements and the company culture). As a result, old methods were, and still are, employed. There is only reason to change if:

- the market changes;
- customers have other wishes and requirements;
- the competitors have become so successful that the operating results come under pressure.

As long as this does not happen, there is no need to change. But when the market changes, most companies are not able to respond quickly enough, and then suffer the consequences. It is for good reason that Darwin's theory is often referred to, which is all about adapting to changes, for which a company does not necessarily need to be the biggest or the strongest. The many start-ups and successful small and medium-sized businesses are good examples of this.

From Buyer Uncertainty to Provider Uncertainty (*Caveat Emptor* Transformation)

Change became necessary when customers started to become more assertive as they were able to gain more access to information. In the old model, *caveat emptor* applied, meaning that the buyer had to be aware of the supplier, the supply and the product. The risk was an ill-suited or disappointing purchase. The customer tried to reduce this uncertainty by buying well-known brands, with warranty conditions, asking the sales staff specific questions or simply trying out the product. The guarantee was a combination of trust in the product and the strength of the sales outlet. In the beginning, this trust in webshops was non-existent, and to this day there is often still some uncertainty regarding the purchase. Consumers still use the Internet to gain information and make comparisons, to acquire more knowledge and consider alternatives. Afterwards, the consumer contacts a distribution point (or shop) and finally decides on a purchase based on trust and the best guarantee. This process is the reverse of the classic pipeline, where the buyer needed protection against a bad buy or faulty products. These days, suppliers deliver products under the condition of a right of return, as a result of which the risk has shifted towards the supplier. The high return percentages show that buyers are abusing this right. Many orders are casually returned, often after the products have actually been used or worn. The supplier then refunds the purchase price. New legislation is clearly needed. Ultimately, the costs of these returns will have to be incorporated within the price. This improper behaviour of buyers is leading to major, uncontrollable risks for the provider. The so called caveat venditor.

The Internet has given customers access to more information and knowledge. As a result, the earlier-mentioned process has taken a sudden and complete turnaround. The customer often has greater knowledge about the product and the product experiences than the actual distribution point or salesperson. In order to compensate for this, it is necessary that sales staff have at least the same level of knowledge (supported, for example, by the company's own information and experience platform), which can be achieved by employing experts on a full-time or on-call basis (Apple, for example, has an expert team at each shop, a service that MediaMarkt (metro) has also recently implemented). What is more, the focus has to shift away from products to the needs of customers, and an appropriate advice should complement this. This is an individual approach, whereby trust is built on the basis of advice, of which the product, of course, forms part. This shift towards *customer first* requires new technology, which is fortunately available (Figure 3).

Due to the adoption of online applications and the ensuing changes such as increased connectivity, decentral production possibilities (3D printing, for example), analysis systems and AI, it is crucial that companies apply these technologies if they are to retain competitive strength. This requires a new value creation model. In marketing, value creation at the contact touchpoint and value exchange applies more than ever. As previously discussed, in the classic model value was created in the supply chain, whereas in the new model value is created at the point of contact.

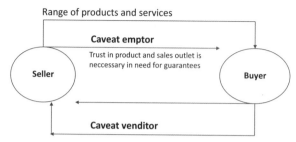

Figure 3.   From *caveat emptor* to *caveat venditor*: a shift in power.

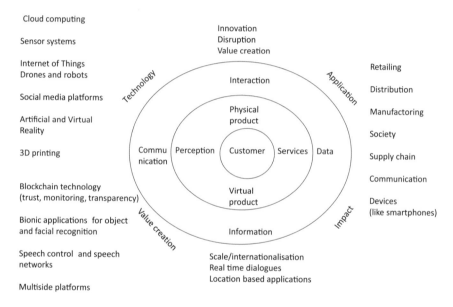

Figure 4.   Relationship between technology, market and customers.

The supply chain is being reduced to a means of distribution whereby links no longer create any added value, but rely upon cost reductions as we have seen in the model of Tracy and Wiersema. This value creation can no longer take place without data (perhaps even big data), nor without information and interaction.

Figure 4 shows on the right-hand side the application in certain trades, and on the left-hand side new technologies. In between are the areas of application. As an example, social media platforms are a new technology which is applied in communication and will lead to a certain perception. It is used to communicate about products to a customer who wants to buy (retailing).

Is Data the Basis for Competitive Strength?

For the competitive strength of an organisation, it is essential to use and analyse data and to act upon it. The moment of purchase must be given optimal support, both physically and via the Internet. Competitive strength then consists of the following:

- transparency in the information process and communication process prior to the sale;
- effective support based on specific data (regarding behaviour, purchase and customer);
- total product concept traditionally from physical product or service, trust and perception;
- unequivocal *touchpoint* experience with an integral application of service, communication, interaction and perhaps physical experience (including hedonism);
- algorithms as a basis for communication and predictions.

But this is not all. How can you bond customers and how can you attract them? This is a growing problem based on the old criteria. Products are comparable, prices are transparent, the supply is unlimited and customers can find all the information, thereby acquiring all the knowledge, they need to make the purchase. What is more, a customer demands evermore personal attention and buys on the basis of personal preferences. This brings about a decline in customer loyalty, and as a result a customer has to constantly be convinced of the appropriateness of his purchase (product based) and the correctness of his choice (distribution point). Due to the large range of products available, the transparency in the market and the many providers, particularly on the Internet, providers are faced with a new competition problem. The distribution point is no longer the end of the supply chain with a customer (at least the transaction) as the last link in the chain; it is with the customer that the buying process begins. As already mentioned, this requires a great deal of knowledge of the customer, the behaviour and motivation for the purchase as there is no future without data. A bond however must also be created between the distribution point and the customers. In the early years of the Internet, this bond was largely product based or supplier based (or for consumers, shop based). This was mainly due to their local presence and the habit of consumers to shop locally or buy from regular suppliers. This has now changed. The Internet has acquired a fully-fledged place in the buying process, and, with each transaction, suppliers have to compete with other providers, often also new start-ups, all over again.

Searching on the Internet does, however, take time. Perhaps in the beginning this was fun, spending an evening surfing the net and making comparisons, but these days this can be a bit of a chore. Google Search resolved this issue, as described earlier, but that was very much based on the classic buying behaviour, searching for products. Customers are increasingly loyal to just a small number of providers. This in turn makes searching on Google for webshops less and less important. Google Search is now actually increasingly being used for looking up information, including product information. For the buying process, the popular web-shops are becoming more important as search engines and attract visitors looking for products and product information. These webshops attract the visitors through trust, *top-of-mind* position and experience. For a limited number of providers, this results in repeating return and buying behaviour. Thanks to the exponential growth in the number of sales on the Internet, these parties will also grow exponentially. The success of these large webshops are measured by the number of visitors, the time they stay on the site, the number of purchases and the increase in the number of purchases and the amount spent per customer. The more purchases per customer in a particular timeframe and the higher the amount, the greater the bonding (see also the RFM analysis). The competition takes place on the basis of the bonding with these groups of buyers. The stronger the bond, the more difficult it is for other providers to compete.

This growth of large websites resulted in the smaller websites finding it increasingly difficult to attract visitors. The smaller ones incurred high costs, for example, with Google and on social media trying to attract customers (SEO and *social media advertising*). Based on the old way of thinking and structure: come to my site. The competition with the large websites such as Zalando, Alibaba and Amazon led to a competitive disadvantage for independent providers. New opportunities arose due to the application of the new possibilities such as Cloud and new programming techniques and application programming interfaces (API). Collaboration became the keyword, i.e., competitive strength through collaboration and direct communication. The large technology companies are the new market leaders thanks to advanced technology and the support possibilities. It is now necessary that all relevant parties collaborate in the platform in order to counterbalance the large webshops that still emerge from the old model. However, these webshops are not sitting quietly but are adapting to the new platform possibilities, particularly as aggregator. Thus, new conflicts are arising. Local municipalities are afraid to lose control of the supply of shops to large peer-to-peer platforms such as Booking.com and Airbnb. And the government is afraid of losing tax revenues, as these large, foreign platforms are creative in finding countries where the tax laws are more favourable. Traditional tax legislation is woefully inadequate in getting these new parties to pay tax, and there is a growing worry about markets that lack competition.

This is all very justified, but the apathy shown by the traditional parties in charge in failing to recognise these developments and to take measures on time have brought this situation about. We see this throughout Europe. An article in the Dutch newspaper *Financieel Dagblad* (23 November 2018) fd.nl/krant/2018/11/23 sets out very clearly how Europe is already far behind in the battle against digital hegemony. This article on the platform economy suggests that the dominance in the platform world comes from platform companies in America and China. An imbalance of power has developed, and Europe only plays a minor role with just 2% of the market value of these companies being European. This was already discussed in my book *De platformstrategie, het wordt buigen of barsten* (*The Platform Strategy; Bend or Break*), 2017. The rules of the play of competition and, for example, contracts (labour) are now determined outside of Europe. The conclusion of this article is crystal clear: speedy action is necessary. The traditional trend cannot be reversed; you either take part or accept the consequences. And this goes for companies as well as local and national governments.

Who Will Become the New Market Leaders?

The new platforms, as described, are becoming the new dominant parties in the market, and will compete against the large webshops. A market, however, will also emerge for niche players who are not able to compete against the large parties, but do disrupt submarkets. This does not involve the universal thinking in terms of target groups of the classic approach, but rather the bonding with specific behaviour and needs-driven target groups. The bond that these niche players have to create with customers comes mainly through communication. The more specific the communication and better targeted the issue, the stronger the bond. You do not win the customers' loyalty through discounts or loyalty points any more, but through services and trust. A relationship is built with communication (Figures 5 and 6).

The value creation of the network and of platforms is based on the following three pillars:

- the shift from a supply focus to a demand focus, from producer to customer;
- the shift from a focus on resources to a focus on the network (ecosystem);
- the shift from value creation in the process (supply chain) to value creation in the interaction.

Figure 5.   Linear business versus platforms and network organisations.

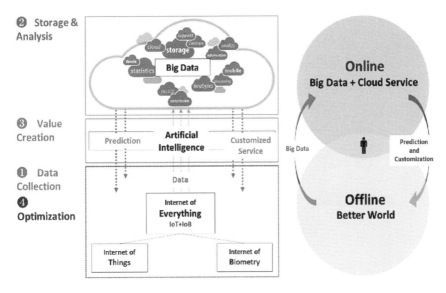

Figure 6.   External system influences on a network organisation.

Industrial Market

As I have mentioned earlier, in recent years, there have been some clear changes in the industrial market. In actual fact, we see a similar development as there has been with other markets: collaboration in a close relationship based on added value. Except with an industrial market there is a production process. Products are usually manufactured in a process that consists of a sequence of links. Each part of this process can be separated, and outsourced, or form an integral part of the total manufacturing process. Then there are the raw materials, auxiliary materials and supply materials. This is a complex process and a complicated business task, and is often even specific to the manufacturer. The control function is important in this entire process. Compare this with, for example, a contractor who manages the construction and coordinates not only the purchasing from various suppliers but also the deliveries. Staff are also hired according to the required specialisation. This is an example of the coordination that is necessary in the industrial market. Platforms can play a role in every part of the process, in the connection with the independent activities and in the management. Platforms such as werkspot.nl and taskrabbit.co.uk

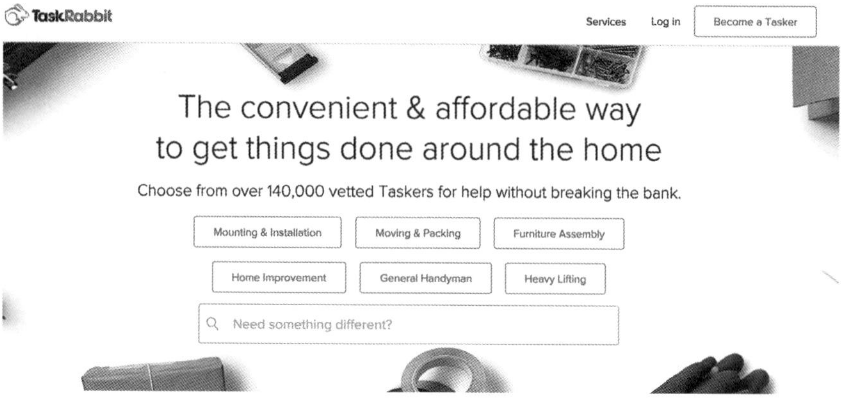

Figure 7.   Example Taskrabbit.co.uk.

are platforms that match freelancers looking for work with the 'providers' of the work (Figure 7). Searches can be carried out on the basis of a worker's specialisation and the sort of work offered. This means that companies no longer have to work with local parties, but can have the individual workers carry out the work; for example, they can subcontract to a plastering company, or hire an individual plasterer.

Platforms in the industrial market have a number of functions, which are as follows:

- Information platforms that can be consulted for specific questions on legislation, constructions, subsidies, problems and often also for consultation with other specialists.
- Platforms that provide access to the supply. These are supply-oriented platforms, which link the various parties on the basis of specific questions, such as building companies, production companies, logistics companies, security companies and suppliers. This creates transparency in the relevant market. These platforms are very user-friendly, have a larger market reach and support a decision-making process. Depending on the success of such a platform, the strength of this platform will either be disruptive or purely supportive (Figure 8).[1]

---

[1] Currier, J. (2018). Platform: Plug and Play.

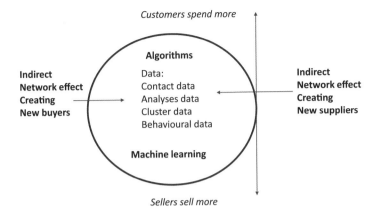

Figure 8.   Network effects.

The network effect of the platforms in every market, also the industrial market, relies on the ability to allow new suppliers to join quickly (based on APIs). The appeal of these platforms can be measured by the number of visitors. Thanks to the popularity of the platform, many different providers can offer their services that can in some way or other be associated with the core of the platform. The driving force behind the network economy is created by generating economies of scale on the demand side of the economy, also known as network effects. These arise when users create value for other users. The larger the network, the richer the data produced by the online interaction between demand and supply, the better the matching functionality of the platform and the more valuable the underlying platform is for users on both sides of the market. This, in turn, attracts more users. The networks effects enable platform companies to grow exponentially instead of linearly as with classic companies. When a linear organisation acquires a new customer, it gains only one new relationship, one extra transaction. In a platform organisation, however, a new consumer can initiate a relationship with all producers on the platform.

The most important competitive advantage of a platform is the network of producers and consumers that creates value for one another and that through the platform enables value to be exchanged.

Are New Market Relationships Also All about Power?

The power is shifting from the provider to the consumer/customer. A provider has to respond to the wishes of the customer and has to wait to see if he is satisfied. With online purchases a customer has up to two weeks to decide whether or not to return the products. There are also different guarantee schemes that apply within platforms. Alibaba (AliExpress), for example, withholds the payment for one month. If there is a complaint from a customer or the articles are returned, the supplier does not receive any payment. It is only once a customer is satisfied that the money is paid out (escrow arrangement). This uncertainty requires an increasing necessity for certainty for the customer and guarantee for the supplier. New guarantee conditions are therefore necessary. This dilemma also forms the basis for new, network-based technologies such as blockchain, analyses, artificial intelligence (AI) and algorithms.

In the old model, the customer was uncertain about the provider (*caveat emptor*). This was typical for the supply economy. In the traditional demand economy, this dependence has undergone a complete reversal. A provider depends on a customer to buy or to specify his needs (*caveat venditor*). The provider then has to wait and see whether the customer is satisfied. If this is not the case, a customer will return the article and ask for his money back. Physical retailers often point this out as an example of unfair competition of Internet providers. This '*caveat venditor*' is, of course, unpleasant for providers who want to fight this by imposing different requirements or by asking buyers for guarantees (B2B market), or through protective activities such as in the case of Zalando.

> Zalando is attaching to some of its clothing range large labels with the text 'do not remove this tag'. The German fashion seller hopes that this will reduce the number of worn items of clothing being returned. The label, measuring 10 × 15 cm, is attached to the outside of mainly eveningwear, such as cocktail dresses and ball gowns. If the label is removed, the article may not be returned. It is not yet clear whether all clothing will be given these anti-return labels. 'We are in the middle of the test phase, so we can't yet say what the impact is on the number of orders returned,' says a spokesperson from Zalando to the Dutch newspaper *Algemeen Dagblad*.

This is quite a remarkable step to take as Zalando's return policy is one of its distinctive selling points. From the very beginning, it allowed items to be returned free of charge, and this right of return was valid for 100 days. 'At the same time, we try to reduce the number of returned clothing items that could have been avoided, through, for example, better product descriptions or presentation', explains the spokesperson. Zalando claims that its return percentage is around fifty percent.[2]

---

[2] *Source*: https://retailtrends.nl/news/55270/zalando-bestrijdt-retouren-met-mega-label-op-kleding.

Chapter 9

Opportunities for Asia Based on Characteristics and Culture

The focus of all major developments is on the United States and the adoption in the Western world. Asia, however, is regarded as the largest evolving market with a growing population and rising wealth. China, for example, has a population of 1.4 billion people, South Korea 51.7 million and Vietnam 95 million. All these countries are developing rapidly in terms of Internet adoption, but the political and cultural differences in the way the Internet is used vary. The business landscape and focus will only add to these differences. The United States is likely to lead the Internet marketing trend, especially for search and communication: transparency. This is due to Google being the leader in search engines, and Facebook and Instagram being the most widely used social media platforms worldwide. This results in billions of users every day seeing many paid ads without even noticing. Moreover, the use of their Ad systems allows users to see more relevant ads based on their needs. This enables marketers to target specific customers easily and accurately, resulting in more marketers promoting their brands on Facebook and Instagram. Data in Table 1 demonstrate the vital role that mobile Internet can play in raising prosperity throughout an area where the incidence of poverty remains high. However, fully exploiting this potential will require a supportive policy environment.

Table 1.   Overview of Southeast Asian country characteristics.

Country	GDP per capita (US$, PPP exchange rate)	Population ('000s)	Urban Density	Mobile Cellular Subscriptions (per 100 Inhabitants)
Brunei	57,770	423	76%	110
Cambodia	3,446	15,578	22%	155
Indonesia	11,019	257,940	55%	126
Laos	5,423	6,802	39%	68
Malaysia	26,812	30,384	76%	149
Myanmar	4,917	53,897	34%	48
Philippines	7,334	100,892	45%	112
Singapore	84,548	5,546	100%	157
Thailand	16,337	67,981	48%	143
Vietnam	5,830	93,448	33%	146

Source: Conclusions of the Oxford Economics report *The Impact of Mobile Internet on the Economy of Southeast Asia*, Oxford Economics, CIA.

It is interesting to compare the applications and possibilities in Southeast Asia with the Western world. In most cases, Southeast Asia not only has its own constraints and limitations but also its own possibilities. In Europe, the privacy laws are strict, and the business rules are formalised and often based on an Anglo-Saxon business model. In the United States, laws are more relaxed and less restrictive. This is one of the reasons why so many new innovations start in the United States. Southeast Asia has a different approach, different political constraints and, above all, a different culture. All the new developments from the West will therefore be adapted to suit the use (social network services (SNS)) in Asia.

Opportunities in Asia

Asia is a global leader in mobile technology, with five out of the global top 10 markets in terms of smartphone penetration. In Southeast Asia, mobile Internet penetration has more than trebled since 2010. It reached 38% in 2014, in line with the global average despite lower incomes in many

Table 2. Smartphone Penetration 2018

Rank ⬍	Country ⬍	Total Population ⬍	Smartphone Penetration ⬍	Smartphone Users ⬍
1	United Arab Emirates	9,543,000	82.2%	7,845,000
2	Sweden	9,987,000	74.0%	7,391,000
3	Switzerland	8,524,000	73.5%	6,268,000
4	South Korea	50,897,000	72.9%	37,114,000
5	Taiwan	23,611,000	72.2%	17,050,000
6	Canada	36,958,000	71.8%	26,531,000
7	United States	328,836,000	71.5%	235,156,000
8	Netherlands	17,085,000	71.0%	12,129,000
9	Germany	80,561,000	71.0%	57,200,000
10	United Kingdom	65,913,000	70.8%	46,639,000

Note: China not included but 78.7% in 2018, young people under 30 almost 100%.

Source: Wikipedia.

countries. See Table 2 for smartphone penetration in 2018. In many Southeast Asian nations, mobile represents the sole means of connecting to the Internet for the majority of the population. Mobile usage has a great impact on one's personal and business life. Communication is the core of existence. In this book, we concentrate on the impact of marketing and mean the 'impact of marketing ON companies'.

With mobile applications people can be reached directly, and companies can sell wherever they want. This will lead to new prosperity in countries and regions that had not been able to compete previously.

> We estimate that advancements in mobile technology since 2010 led to regional GDP being US $47.2 billion (1.9 percent) higher than it would otherwise have been by 2015. By way of context, this is equivalent to the increase in GDP of the entire financial services industry during this period.[1]

The impact of the Internet and mobile applications will not only lead to higher GDP and more income for people (and increased spending power) but also to new business activities. New and existing companies can make

---

[1] *Source*: *Oxford Economics*, The impact of Mobile Internet on the Economy of SE Asia.

their processes more efficient, but above all expand their markets. Companies like Alibaba and JD.com can not only create a strong "home market" in Asia but also a strong market position abroad. These companies are so strong in Asia (particularly China) that it is hard for foreign companies to compete.

> Amazon has finally given up the fight with Chinese online shopping giants to capture the domestic market. On Thursday, the Seattle-based e-commerce company announced it will shut down its marketplace on Amazon.cn, which connects mainland Chinese buyers and sellers, while other units of its local venture will stay intact.
>
> The partial retreat, first reported by Reuters and Bloomberg, is indicative of the relentless e-commerce race in China where Alibaba and JD.com dominate, with newcomer Pinduoduo closing on the incumbents' heels.[2]

This example shows that a strong home market is a good defence against foreign companies. Home-based companies have the right culture, and understand the language, behaviour, laws and the impact of communication. Based on a low pricing structure, a large home market and a young workforce, Asia has a strong competitive advantage which will lead to a higher GDP and a strong competitive force. New developments, as described in this book, will lead to even more changes and opportunities. The Western world is overregulated, and companies are restricted by their existing structures. The Anglo-Saxon business model with a strong focus on short-term profit and stock values is no longer the best strategy. This will lead to new opportunities for Asia.

> **Sale Stock** is a rapidly growing startup that breathes data and technology in its core business. Sale Stock, an Indonesian online fashion goods retailer, was launched in September 2014 and has since undergone considerable expansion. It now employs more than 500 people in six offices and has plans to double its workforce in the near future. It owes its existence to the rise of mobile technology. Sale Stock is almost entirely geared to the use of mobile Internet with some 90 percent of visitors coming

---

[2] *Source:* Techcrunch.com (18 April 2019).

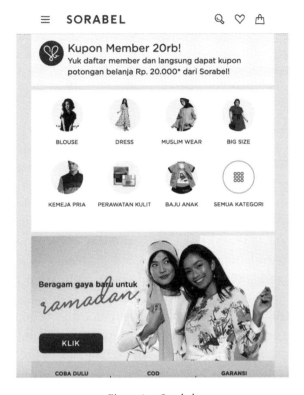

Figure 1.   Sorabel.

through this source. By making use of mobile as a direct route to customers it is able to offer affordable fashion at lower prices and to a much larger customer base than its bricks-and-mortar competitors.[3]

In 2019, Sale Stock changed its name to Sorabel, as it entered its fifth year of operations.

According to an official statement by the company on its blog, the name Sorabel comes from Soraya and the French word for beauty — *belle*. The rebranding was meant to strengthen the company's mission to provide fashion products for its mainly female customers, who are nicknamed 'sista' (Figure 1).

---

[3] *Source*: Oxford Technology, The Impact of Mobile on SE Asia.

The rebranding will soon be followed by changes to the company's website and app, including the name and logo on its social media presence. Users currently visiting the Sale Stock websites will be redirected to Sorabel. Its app on Play Store has also been changed to Sorabel.[4]

New Opportunities Based on Social Media

Social media is important in Southeast Asia and China. The mobile phone is the major reason behind the growth of e-commerce in all its aspects. As we have seen previously, the mobile phone will lead to more interaction, more commerce and all in all to a higher GPD. The mobile phone enjoys high adoption rates among young people. Because of the history of China and Southeast Asia, the number of young people and the domination of the young as employees and customers are higher than in the Western world. **60% of the world youth population lives in Asia.** This offers a great opportunity for Internet use as the adoption of new technology is higher among young people than with any other age group. Young people are more adaptable, do not have responsibilities or fixed structures and are less constrained. Moreover, the size of the young population also offers the opportunity to test new developments before "going to market". Test groups of millions are possible without disrupting existing markets.

Secondly, these young people can be trained and educated to use new insights and technology like the fourth industrial revolution opportunities. It can be embedded in the education systems and lead to better jobs and greater employment opportunities. In this case, Asia will become leader in applying and marketing new technology and new business opportunities. Platforms started in Asia; Alibaba was the initiator of new business concepts and a new approach to platforms and the Internet. This is not a coincidence but the consequence of less restrictions, a government that recognises opportunities and the slow uptake of new technology in the Western world. And this process has only just started (Figure 2).

---

[4] *Source*: e27.co.

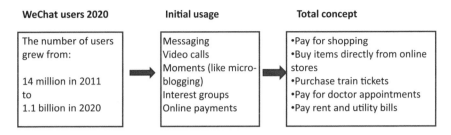

Figure 2. Number of monthly active WeChat users from Third Quart (in millions).

But today, as Asia celebrates its 50th anniversary, the world stands on the cusp of the Fourth Industrial Revolution, driven by technologies such as artificial intelligence, machine learning, autonomous vehicles, ubiquitous mobile Internet, and accelerating progress in genetics, materials science and ultra-cheap automation. If Asia is to prosper for another 50 years, it must tackle difficult questions about how to navigate the accelerating pace of technological change and digital disruption. The Fourth Industrial Revolution could bring huge benefit to the region, driving financial inclusion, access to affordable healthcare, new forms of education, and the creation of new companies and service sector jobs.

Asia is today the fastest growing Internet market in the world. A recent report from Google and Temasek calculates that the region's online population is expanding by 124,000 new users every day — and will continue at this pace for the next five years. Equally, however, technology could cause many challenges. As robots become ever cheaper, can manufacturing still be a route to job creation? How should the region teach IT and technology skills and create a vibrant innovation ecosystem? How can governments build the right enabling environment, and a connected regional digital economy, that enables the Fourth Industrial Revolution to thrive?[5]

---

[5] *Source:* https://www.straitstimes.com/asia/se-asia/youth-technology-and-growth-will-determine-aseans-future.

HIGHLIGHTS

• Youth make up about 19% of the region's total population.

• Over 60% of the world's youth live in Asia-Pacific. This translates into more than 750 million young women and men aged 15 to 24 years.

• Significant strides have been made with respect to educational attainment. The region is on track to meet MDG 2 on universal primary education. Net enrolment in secondary education has also been steadily increasing and is now at 64.1%, slightly above the world average of 62.5%.

• Transition to the labour market remains a major challenge as youth unemployment is more than double the rate of the total working age population. The proportion of adolescent and youth migrants in the total international migrant population is 19% in Asia and 13% in the Pacific, most of them are women.

• Gender inequalities have been reduced at all education levels, primary, secondary and tertiary, with the exception of some countries. Young women, however, are underrepresented in the labour market, and are thus an untapped resource for future economic growth and development.

• Rates of adolescent childbearing have dropped significantly in most countries of Asia and the Pacific in the past two to three decades, but they still remain high.

The Asia-Pacific region contains 60 per cent of the world's youth population, or 750 million young persons aged 15 to 24 years. In 2010, India alone had 234 million young people, the highest number of any country in the world (representing 19 per cent of the country's total population), followed by China with 225 million (representing 17 per cent of the total population). By comparison, Japan only had 12 million young people or 10 per cent of the population. Bangladesh and the Philippines both also had very high shares of youth – around 20 per cent of the total population.[1]

Asia-Pacific youth have benefitted from the region's social and economic dynamism. Youth unemployment remains the lowest among all regions of the world, at 11 per cent. Secondary and tertiary education enrolment rates have also increased to 64.1 and 25.3 per cent respectively.[2]

Nevertheless, significant numbers of youth across the region still face a variety of obstacles in their access to employment, education and healthcare. Transition between education and employment is one of the main obstacles facing youth of the region, especially those from South and South-West Asia, South-East Asia and the Pacific. Access to adequate healthcare is also hampered by

---

[1] United Nations World Population Prospects, the 2010 Revision. Available online at: http://esa.un.org/wpp/
[2] ESCAP Statistical Yearbook, 2012. Available online at: http://www.unescap.org/stat/data/syb2012/

 http://undesadspd.org/Youth.aspx    facebook.com/UN4Youth    twitter.com/UN4Youth

The answer is collaboration. This collaboration is not only between companies to offer goods and services through a platform like Airbnb or Alibaba but also in close cooperation with the government and financial

institutions. Platforms will create an efficient business environment through the links within the network economy because it is based on customer needs. The platforms communicate directly with their users and can offer a wide variety of products and services through linked suppliers. The cloud is the facilitator, but application programming interfaces (APIs) are interfaces that will make connections possible. A platform therefore does not have big storage rooms, large offices or other constraints from the physical world and classic business models. By linking suppliers through APIs, a large number of suppliers can sell through the platform. The platform is the marketing engine for attracting customers and matching customer needs with the offerings of suppliers (or linking supplier with other suppliers). Because of the marketing power of platforms and the unlimited number of suppliers, exponential growth is possible. Asian businesses can export their unique selling points like low-priced products, extra services and special made products on a world scale. This will be a great economic boost with employment at places that were not possible before and selling to countries that had previously been out of reach. Asia can create competitive advantages over the Western world because of the region's ability to use technology and to change the rules of competition.

Mobile broadband has proved to be a vital tool for the company, enabling it to reach a broader range and number of customers very rapidly and to have a major impact on the efficiency of its operations. The mobile Internet means Thanh Ly Hang Cu is able to deliver consumers lower prices and better services, as well as create wealth and jobs for Vietnam (Figure 3).

Technology Impact

New revolutionary technology, like blockchain, cloud and micro services, is the future of storing and sharing information, as well as completing transactions. The proclivity of Southeast Asian citizens to rapidly adopt new technology and the number of new start-ups providing blockchain solutions in the region such as mobile, banking and shopping create huge economic potential for technology companies based in Asia. The potential to become world leaders will make Asia an important hotspot.

Figure 3.   Thanh Ly Hang Cu produces new office furniture and also trades in second-hand and clearance furniture across Vietnam.

SINGAPORE — Southeast Asians are outpacing the Chinese in embracing the mobile economy, with higher percentages of the population in several countries using smartphones to do their banking, to shop and hail rides.

China may be home to giant e-tailers like Alibaba Group Holding, but Indonesia has the world's highest mobile e-commerce penetration rate, a new report reveals. Thailand leads the way in mobile banking penetration, while Singapore is ride-hailing central — two fields in which China doesn't even crack the top five.

The findings explain why investment money is steadily pouring into Southeast Asian startups. That money is fueling a digital revolution that has already made the region one of the world's most powerful growth drivers, while China grapples with a worsening slowdown.

Among Thailand's Internet users, 74% access banking services via mobile devices, according to the annual Global Digital Report 2019 from social media management platform Hootsuite and digital marketing agency We Are Social. That puts one of Asia's favourite vacation spots well ahead of the global rate of 41% and higher than China, at 61%.

Home to South East Asia's largest ride-hailing service provider, Singapore is No. 1 in the world when it comes to people grabbing taxis via a mobile app. © Reuters.

Indonesia, home to e-commerce unicorns Tokopedia and Bukalapak, topped the world in mobile e-commerce usage. In the past month, 76% of its Internet users bought something via a mobile device. In this category, the archipelago known more for its seismic activity leaves the rest of the world, at 55%, in the dust and even beats China, at 74%. The country's demographics seem tailor made for mobile e-commerce. About 60% of the 260 million Indonesians are under 40. Mobile penetration is at 70% and accessing the Internet with a smartphone is the norm. Mobile e-commerce is especially popular in cities, where shopping online also buys time and a detour around mind-numbing gridlock.[6]

Impact of Technology

In Asia, 60% of the population is younger than 35 (total population is 6.4 billion). They are young, dynamic, very modern and communicative with their own culture. "Always online" is not too much of an exaggeration. It is almost strange to see a young person walking on the street without a telephone. Huawei is the region's own, very popular brand. Mutual communication takes place via the variant of WhatsApp: WeChat.

---

[6] *Source*: https://asia.nikkei.com/Business/Business-trends/Southeast-Asia-eclipses-China-as-world-s-mobile-economy-hot-spot.

However, WeChat is more all-encompassing than WhatsApp, the West's communication app. Everything is linked on the basis of WeChat, from visiting a hospital to insurance, and from buying tickets to contacting the government. WeChat is the central point that records everything. This is an ideal position as platform where data can be used to give personal services linked with suppliers. This not only naturally creates an optimal service for users but also an unprecedented dependence because everything, including all government contacts such as a driver's licence or passport, is linked to this. The number of Tencent's WeChat active accounts from the second quarter of 2010 to the first quarter of 2018 is impressive. In the most recently reported quarter, Tencent's WeChat had 1,040 million monthly active users.

> Tencent uses WeChat as the centre for all its services. Tencent is a totally integrated platform, a so-called multisided platform, where users can share messages, videos and products. Interactivity is supported. Tencent calls itself a "social network platform", and with a market share of 69% it is by far the largest. CtoC facilities via "QQ" and "moments" are impressive for gaming, video sharing and shopping. JD.com, one of the largest sales platforms in China, claims that 60% of purchases come through WeChat users. Total market share of online sales 16.3% compared to Alibaba 58.2% (July 2018). Of course, all the numbers are impressive, certainly for people outside Asia, but I am struck by the infrastructure that has been laid down, the integration of data and activities and the algorithms. An automatic communication process based on the behaviour of users, where customization is possible for every user.

Asia, especially China, not only has a clear competitive weapon, namely the low wages (unskilled labour), but also the increasing prosperity and free spending opportunities of the young target group. There are no real big industries that make their own products, but China is good at using its resources for simple tasks. Assembly is an example of this (as with iPhones and cars). China is becoming an indispensable link for Western manufacturers for these technical products. The low wages in particular are a decisive factor in this (resource allocation). In South Korea, a strong car manufacturing industry is competing against Japan and Germany. Their cars are of high quality and attractively priced. In this

Regional platforms: **Asia**	Integrated platforms	Multisided platforms
Baidu	Google	Airbnb
Tencent	Apple	Uber
USA	Amazon	Lyft
eBay	Facebook	Takeaway (home food delivery)
Yahoo	Alibaba	
Special purpose		
PayPal		
LinkedIn		
Uber		
Airbnb		
Transaction-based	Multipurpose	Multisided platforms

Figure 4. Platform companies by region.

way, a strong focus of assembly and low-skilled labour is transformed into ready products. Higher paid and higher priced. Also, new industries like telecom are important for Asia. Samsung and Huawei are strong leaders and can compete with all Western industries. In some cases, like Samsung (a wide range of interlinked products) and Huawei (5G networks), the industries are leading the way, leaving the Western world to look for a good defence strategy. Asian commitment and dedication combined with technical knowhow are strong competition tools. New technologies such as cloud computing, networks, platforms and algorithms are also effective tools in the competitive battle. It is clear that the late adoption of Internet technologies in Asia is now working to Asia's advantage (Figure 4).

The Battle of Platforms

There is the impression that the Chinese online market is dominated by a few large online marketplaces, but competition is increasingly coming from small specialised platforms that serve a niche market. The competition no longer takes place on the basis of its own proposition, but on the basis of the power of the platform. Platforms compete with one another due to differences in service provision and bonding factor. Many Chinese people use different platforms.

Developments in China are going so fast that already 42% of worldwide e-commerce sales are taking place in China, with the United States as the world's number 2 with a 24% market share. Purchases can be made at any time and place. Integrated business models, such as that of the HEMA (China), support smartphone use. QR codes are the connecting factor between online and offline at every level. This puts China ahead of the rest of the world. This is the problem of the inhibiting lead of the West, where most Internet applications are based on a desktop computer, later also with a mobile variant. China, and the rest of Asia, has mainly taken the mobile variant as the basis for Internet applications.

Also on media, social media and classical media, there is a strong development of platforms. Platforms like azzhibo.com and zhibo8.cc offer a wide variety of videos and TV channels. Also, WeChat and WeChat Moments are important platforms. Especially, Moments can be used to share information about products and sell the products to your "friends". I saw this happening in Nepal where young Asian girls were taking photos of products that they would share on "Moments". Friends like to buy, particularly for each other. They negotiated with the salespeople and bought the articles in bulk. By selling it for a higher price they actually made more profit than the original salespeople.

Top Quality for Young People

Asia is a vigorously growing market based on young people and mobile technology.

China applies a clear rule for the production of its own products. In most cases, the products do not have to be 100% quality. Often 80% of the top quality is sufficient. Because of the low wages they can offer this 80% quality for 60% of the price. This makes competition almost impossible for European companies, webshops and the physical stores. But why compete on price; the Chinese appreciate European products precisely because of their quality and reliability. Selling in Europe is not even the goal for Chinese companies, it is more like a by-catch of the English-language website. Their own market is developing rapidly and there will be a new elite layer of young people with money, as described earlier, who will set higher demands. European brands are a clear identification of wealth and success. This new elite want European brands, and can also pay for them. This explains, for example, the many Chinese people at the outlet centres in, for instance, Roermond (the Netherlands). Due to increasing domestic demand, Chinese platforms such as Alibaba and J.D.com want to start selling these Western products. Because of this preference, there is a strong focus on attracting European companies to sell via a Chinese platform (especially given the political tensions with the United States). It is not for nothing that Alibaba has an office in Amsterdam to attract European companies and to help them sell their products in China.

> WeChat (Chinese name: Weixin 微信) is one of the most popular messaging apps in Asia, especially in China. The platform was developed by Chinese technology conglomerate Tencent in 2011 and currently it has more than 697 million monthly active users.
>
> Although many western marketers who are trying to expand their business in Asia realize the importance of WeChat, the messaging app can seem daunting, not least of all because of the language barrier. Here, we break down the three three critical components of the app — Moments, Subscriptions and Wallet — and why they matter to brands and publishers.[7]

WeChat's Moments?

Moments (朋友圈) is a fundamental feature of WeChat. There, you can post text-based updates, upload up to nine images as well as share videos and articles, just like your Facebook Timeline or Twitter News Feed. But it differs from those social networks in that Moments offers a higher level of intimacy and privacy: Your contact list is not visible to others; your updates can only be seen by friends who are verified by you; and you can only see the interactions of people on your contact list. For example, if you post a photo and your friend comments on it with an obscene joke, you do not need to worry that your other friends will see this comment — unless they are also friends with the profane jester.

---

[7] *Source*: digiday.com.

South Korea

Target marketing in South Korea

Although the current marketing draws attention to the use of Big Data, data usage in South Korea is significantly low compared to other countries (Choi, 2016). As mentioned previously, targeting specific customers is now possible with SNS, and search engines. However, SNS and search engines in South Korea have no tool to define the target audience due to the lack of data analysis capabilities. This means that marketers can only display advertisements to all users of the SNS and search engines without defining specific customer groups.

In this sense, target marketing in South Korea appeared to have differences from the current target marketing method. Therefore, types of SNS and search engines will be briefly introduced as well as target marketing status to determine the main differences from the current target marketing.

Usage of SNS in South Korea

Fashion and beauty industries have quickly caught on to the trend of the younger generation spending significant amounts of time on social media platforms such as Instagram, Facebook, Twitter and YouTube, rather than on traditional advertising platforms like TV.

A 2017 survey by statistics portal Statista found that 84% of South Koreans were active social media users.

Another set of statistics showed that an average of 2 hours and 15 minutes per day is spent on social networks globally.

As for Instagram, 90% of its users are younger than 35, and 68% are female, according to US social media marketing firm Dreamgrow.

This has led to more brands turning to influencer marketing to lure consumers, further boosting the power of social media stars.

'Influencer marketing has more focus on influential people rather than the target market as a whole. It identifies the individuals with influence, and orients marketing activities around these influencers,' Ms Park Kyung-a, chief executive of mobile marketing and advertising company Stella, told *The Korea Herald*.

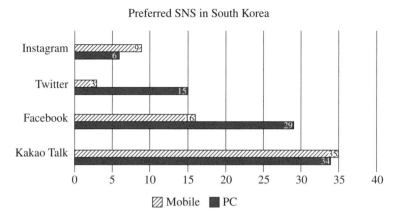

Figure 5.   Preferred SNS to get purchase information (Panjala, 2018).

'Followers of these influencers are more than fans who like celebrities since they not only gain useful information from them but also empathise, communicate and share common interests with influencers,' Ms Park said.

Although Facebook and Instagram are popular across cultures, South Koreans are not particularly enthusiastic about them. They use their own multiplatform texting application called KakaoTalk. The most popular social media platform in the country can be found in Figure 5.

As seen from Figure 5, KakaoTalk is the most popular application to get purchase information among South Koreans, followed by Facebook. However, the preferred SNS is different for each age group.

KakaoTalk is widely used in all age groups, but Facebook is mainly used in the 20s age group. According to Yoon's (2017) study, only 11% of people in the age groups of 40–50 used Facebook, while 30% of those surveyed used Facebook in their 20s. People between the ages of 40 and 50 used social media called Naver Band and KakaoStory (Yoon, 2017). About 20% of people between the ages of 40 and 50 used Naver Band and KakaoStory, but these social media were rarely used among the age group of 20.

This implies that each age group has their preferred SNS to obtain information. One possible reason for this phenomenon is that older users prefer a more closed network because of privacy concerns and they trust the South Korean website that they are familiar with (Yoon, 2017).

Since each age group has a preferred SNS, marketers should first identify their target age range. Most importantly, they need to understand why each age group prefers a particular SNS, so they can create the contents more effectively.

KakaoTalk

Brief introduction and advertising methods

KakaoTalk began as a messenger service where users could chat in real time to one another and/or within groups (Jang and Youn, 2014). In the meantime, it has become Kakao Corporation, which offers 20 different apps. Kakao has three different platforms, on which marketers can effectively promote their products. For marketers, the Kakao platforms are ideal for addressing customers of all ages. On average, South Koreans spend 850 minutes a month on KakaoTalk compared to 28 minutes a month on Facebook Messenger (Medium, 2017). Kakao has raised $90 million to develop its own blockchain network called Klatyn, and the integration of a crypto wallet into KakaoTalk is one way to introduce their own blockchain network to the public.

> Kakao is providing various services such as KakaoStyle, KakoPage, KakaoMusic, etc. and it is expected to further expand its services (Han and Cho, 2015). This will attract not only more Kakao users but also advertisers who consider active interactions and communications on Kakao platforms important in promoting their products or services. Marketers are exposed to more platform options which allow them to display their ads to the most relevant services. DATA has partnered with GroundX, the official blockchain platform of Kakao (Korea's largest social media company), for incubating the blockchain App Antube. Antube is a blockchain-based mobile video community that combines DATA's wallet, SDK and M3 mobile decentralized distributed storage framework, allowing users to mine coins based on the effective attention spent on viewing mobile ads and videos. "Value your moments", Antube will share the ecological value and profit through blockchain technology to the effective contributors in the ecosystem.[8]

---

[8] *Source*: www. medium.com.

Unlike Google and Facebook, Kakao does not utilise a sophisticated algorithm to collect, aggregate and analyse data. There is a wide range of services, so customer groups are automatically divided according to their needs. In other words, without the Big Data base and the technical algorithm, marketers are able to perform traditional target advertising on specific and differentiated platforms. However, as Kakao is still one step behind the current target marketing, marketers still need to select and target some profitable customers. It is problematic in a rapidly changing world as marketers cannot respond quickly to changing patterns of demand. Therefore Kakao, has established a big data platform and is a leading platform for analysing and using data.

News feed advertising on KakaoStory

KakaoStory is one of the services of Kakao Corporation that works in a similar way to Facebook and is particularly popular among the age group of 30–40 years old (mainly females). It is a social networking service where users can share photos and express their emotions in their feed in a more closed network (Johnson, 2017). This service is mainly used by people between the ages of 30 and 40, especially mothers sharing their lives with kids (babies) and selling kids-related products. It is integrated with KakaoTalk and, as a result, users can easily import their contact list from KakaoTalk to KakaoStory.

Advertisers can launch hyper-targeted advertising campaigns through users' feeds (Johnson, 2017). Users can see their advertising campaigns while scrolling down their feeds. As users can share advertising content with one another, advertisers can expect favourable effects through sharing. However, sharing is the biggest advantage marketers can get through KakaoStory. As with TV commercials, advertisers can only target people who have seen their advertising campaigns, so they cannot exactly choose and advertise to people who might be interested in their products and services.

Social media advertising on Naver Band

This service is offered by Naver, which is the most popular search engine in South Korea. Naver Band began by giving users the opportunity to connect with their long-lost alumni and friends (Ok, 2011). It became a public SNS for users to find and join any Band that they are interested in. Users of the Band can share everyday affairs and thoughts within the Band to which they belong (Jang and Youn, 2014). In addition, the Band offers various services such as instant messaging, schedule management, photo and video sharing, etc.

Marketers can target Band users by displaying their brands on Band's main page. Customised advertising is not possible, but they can induce users to click on their Band at a specific time. They need to present their brands in the most appealing way to attract customers. After advertising, they can then analyse the number of clicks to see how many users have become members of their Band. As with KakaoStory, they cannot exactly reach their target group, so they should not expect a successful advertising effect from the Band.

Naver

As already mentioned, target marketing through Google and Facebook is gaining popularity worldwide. These two platforms offer specific information based on individual needs. This means that marketers can promote their products to the customers who are more willing to purchase, which also helps them spend marketing expenses more efficiently (WordStream. com, 2018a,b).

However, South Korea does not have these types of platforms. Marketers should approach their customers differently, as analysing customer data is difficult in South Korea. Most marketers attract users by displaying many ads on the most popular search engine, called Naver. They still believe that targeting the main users of Naver will work better.

What does Naver do?

Naver is the most popular search engine in South Korea, offering a wide range of services (Ok, 2011). Naver is easily accessible with useful information from its huge database of individual blogs, café (Internet communities), shopping public forms, news and multimedia content (Ok, 2011). Naver's homepage resembles the image in Figure 6. Recently, Naver

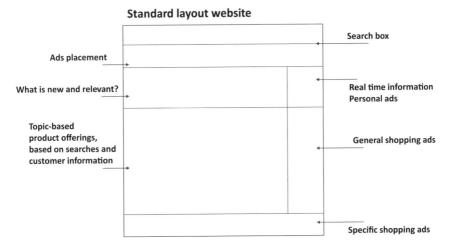

Standard layout website

Search box

Ads placement

What is new and relevant?

Real time information
Personal ads

Topic-based
product offerings,
based on searches and
customer information

General shopping ads

Specific shopping ads

Figure 6.   Naver homepage (Lee, 2018).

launched Smart Store platform to help start-up sellers to sell their products and reach customers. They charge no commission fee to sellers for a year to help them improve cash flow, etc. So, most of Koreans have a mart store; it is really easy and many people use it to sell their products, as well as to start their own business.

'Naver's Smartstore online shop is a platform where business owners can promote and sell their products. The store also helps them to better manage customer relationships,' Naver CEO Han Seong-sook said during the opening ceremony of the Naver Partner Square support center in the southwest city of Gwangju, Thursday. 'By providing them with Naver's technology and data, we will support them to grow their businesses.'

Not only providing an offline platform, the company also announced various support programs that would be helpful for start-ups when selling their products. Introducing its 'Start Zero Commission Fee Program,' Naver said it will not charge any commission fee on sellers at Smart store.

Choi In-hyuk, chief operating officer of Naver, said the company decided to start this program because 'only 27 percent of its online store can sell their products to customers while the other 73 percent just gave up their businesses due to various kinds of obstacles."[9]

As mentioned in Figure 6, there is a number of ad placements where marketers can display their brands. Naver urges users to click on these displayed ads. Sometimes, people visit Naver for market search purposes and, as a result, end up purchasing products. This is one of Naver's strategies. It makes sure that users click on and buy products before they make a search in the search field.

As with other SNS systems in South Korea, these displayed ads are not customised which suggests that everyone who is accessing Naver at the same time sees the same advertisements. Marketers should carefully consider the position of their ads because it costs about €5,000 to advertise on the Naver search engine for a week (Saedu.naver.com, 2018). Ads are displayed to Naver's users who may or may not be interested in the advertiser's products or services. If marketer's ads are exposed to people who are not interested in their product, then their marketing costs are spent inefficiently. This is similar to the traditional way of target marketing because while there are people interested in the advertiser's products, there is no way of knowing about their brand if they have not seen their ads.

Advertising method: Keyword

There is another type of advertising that can be done through Naver, namely keyword advertising. This is aimed at users who are interested in specific keywords. South Koreans rely on Naver to gather information since Naver understands keywords and delivers the most relevant results (Krush, n.d.). For instance, carrying out a search on the Naver search engine will generate results based on the exact match of the search terms. Thus, marketers choosing the most relevant keywords related to their website can expect positive effects.

As shown in Figure 7, there is a keyword tool that marketers can use to manage their keyword ads. To explain in more detail, marketers can select five keywords that are most relevant to their brand and products.

---

[9] *Source*: http://www.koreatimes.co.kr/www/tech/2018/12/133_255509.html.

연관키워드 조회 결과 (920개) **Related Keywords (920 Results)**

전체추가		연관키워드 ⑦	⬍
추가	홍콩마카오페리	Hong Kong Macau Ferry	
추가	홍콩2박3일	Hong Kong 3 Days 2 Nights	
추가	홍콩가볼만한곳	Places To Go In Hong Kong	
추가	홍콩여행	Hong Kong Travel	
추가	2박3일홍콩여행	3 Days 2 Nights Hong Kong Travel	
추가	홍콩자유여행	Hong Kong Independent Travel	
추가	홍콩디즈니랜드	Hong Kong Disneyland	
추가	3박4일홍콩여행	4 Days 3 Nights Hong Kong Travel	
추가	홍콩마카오3박4일	Hong Kong Macau 4 Days 3 Nights	

Figure 7.   Naver keyword analysis tool (Lee, 2018).

These selected keywords can be changed monthly, and advertisers can collect data about the monthly click volume and the number of ads displayed to users. Additionally, they can see the search volume trends with the demographic data. However, the keyword tool only counts the volume of searches and clicks. It does not contain any specific information about the actual users. Naver cannot identify users' historical search or behaviour data, which suggests that marketers cannot identify potential or current customers. This is a drawback of keyword advertising on Naver, but it would be effective if their business requires a lot of research.

Interpretations from South Korea's online advertising

Similarly, to the traditional target marketing, advertisers can promote their brands to the users of the South Korean search engine and the SNS as a whole. Targeting in a more personalised and customised way is not yet popular due to the lack of Big Data analysis capabilities (Choi, 2016). In addition, Kakao is an adequate platform for promoting brands for all age groups, as Kakao users are gradually increasing (Statista, 2018a).

South Korean companies should, however, try to use Big Data to cope with the era of the Fourth Industrial Revolution and to be able to compete with global firms. Failure to analyse data and target specific customers shows that marketing costs are being used inefficiently. South Koreans should therefore develop data analysis capabilities in order to spend marketing costs more effectively and to better understand customer needs.

China

Introduction to China's marketing strategy

China has a unique, dynamic and active social media industry with the world's biggest Internet-user base. A massive volume of data in combination with highly advanced technology has changed the communication and interaction between customers and companies. Due to this, more local and global companies exploit enormous opportunities through social media marketing in China. Both SNS and search engines in China are currently in a position to outcompete global social media including Google and Facebook, through technologies and strategies (Chiu *et al.*, 2015).

Social media in China

Social media in China presents somewhat different characteristics from the United States and South Korea. It is worth mentioning that China's social media is the most active in the world comprising 513 million Internet users whereas the USA has 245 million users (Chiu *et al.*, 2012). This is an advantage as it allows more sophisticated target marketing using customer-based data. What is more, due to the distrust and scepticism about high-level authorities and governmental organisations, the purchasing behaviour of Chinese customers is more influenced by the content on social media. In fact, more than 60% of Chinese people value and appreciate the recommendations of friends and family members on social media, meaning that social media is now deeply embedded in people's daily lives (Tu, 2016). Moreover, there are dominant local SNS and search engines with distinct strengths and strategies (Chiu *et al.*, 2012). From a marketer's point of view, this is important as the social media sector in China is more complex and requires significant understanding and expertise. In order to understand how target marketing is achieved in China, a closer look will be taken at Baidu and WeChat.

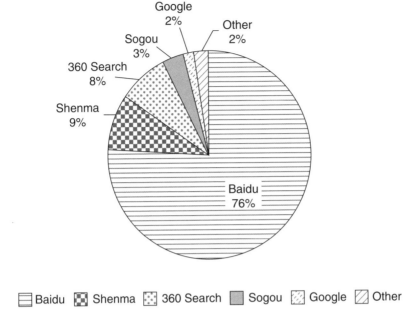

Figure 8.   Search engine market in China in 2017 (China Whisper, 2018).

Baidu

Founded in 2000, Baidu is the biggest search engine in China, and has 76% of the total search engine market share in China (China Whisper, 2018). It provides more than 110 services such as Baidu Baike (music service), Baidu Wangpan (cloud service) and Baidu Wallet (financial services), attracting 665 million mobile search users every month (Baidu, 2016). Figure 8 shows the statistics of the search engine market in China.

Rich data for target marketing

Baidu has an active online environment for effective target marketing thanks to the enormous volume of data. The database contains extensive information collected from large user groups and 300,000 websites (Marketing to China, 2018). A wide range of data from location-based to query-based information enables the targeting of different customer groups. For example, search data gives information about users' long-term search patterns, access patterns to certain websites and web surfing data (Baidu, 2018). Based on this Big Data, companies and retailers understand customer needs by identifying purchasing patterns and the online experiences of customers. This all leads to successful marketing strategies. For instance, a partnership between Baidu and P&G allowed P&G to uncover customer needs by exploring the search patterns of Chinese users on Baidu. Based on Baidu Knows, where users proactively ask questions and share experiences, significant concern about aging and skin conditions was revealed among the customer group of middle-aged women. This gave P&G insights into the specific target group of middle-aged women so it could produce an advertisement with the slogan of "hold on to age 25" (Chiu *et al.*, 2015).

There are four advertising channels where marketers can target certain customer groups: Pay Per Click (PPC), Baidu Union (Display Network) and Baidu Brand Zone.

Pay Per Click (PPC)

Baidu Pay Per Click is effective in advertising brand/service/products only to those who show interest by searching related keywords. As an advertiser, there are ways to control ads to target certain audiences. For example, "day-part targeting" specifically controls when ads are displayed (Baidu Advertising, 2018). Depending on the target customer, advertisers can arrange ads by specifying working hours, the day of the week, time of day, etc. Furthermore, "geographic targeting" allows marketers to target their customers based on location, either local or overseas, or a specific region in China (Baidu Advertising, 2018). However, given that most of Baidu users are located in China, targeting customers overseas does not usually seem attractive. For "keyword match type", marketers can decide whether keywords that customers search, should be broadly matched, phrase-matched or exactly matched in order for ads to be displayed (Baidu Advertising, 2018). To have advertisements exposed at the very top, marketers need to bid just like with Google's advertisements (Figure 9).

Baidu Union (display network)

There are more than 300,000 websites affiliated to Baidu which are subdivided into industry categories and brands (Marketing China, 2018).

What is Baidu?

Baidu, Inc. operates as an internet search provider, which offers internet search solutions and online marketing solutions. The firm operates as an e-commerce platform with an online payment tool, develops and markets web application software, and provides human resource related services. It operates through the following segments: Search Services, Transaction Services and iQiyi. The Search Services segment includes the traditional search engine related businesses such as auction-based P4P services and display-based online advertising services. The Transaction Services segment includes the newly developed internet businesses such as services provided by Baidu Nuomi, takeout delivery services and other online-to-offline services. The iQiyi segment engages in the online video business. The company was founded by Yanhong Li and Xu Yong on January 18, 2000 and is headquartered in Beijing, China.

Why Baidu?

In the United States is Google.
In China, they have Baidu.
If you're wondering, "what does this have to do with me?" I get it. What does China's biggest tech company have to do with you?
A lot, if you're involved with marketing and SEO.
Take a look, for instance, at this stunning fact: 90% of online search queries done in China are done through Baidu.
This amounts to billions of searches per month!

Figure 9.   Baidu more than a service engine.

Baidu Union's advertising targets potential customers under a certain industry category. For instance, if a perfume company tries to advertise their new men's perfume product line, they can focus on the 'men's cosmetics' category and the company's product will pop up on every website related to men's cosmetics. Just like PPC advertising, marketers can choose target customers by choosing a location, age group, time, etc. Baidu Union advertising includes not only text links but also other visually attractive formats such as banner, videos, and other rich media (Sampi, 2018).

Baidu Brand Zone

Baidu Brand Zone displays advertisements of brands on the top of the Search Engine Results Page (SERP) in five ways. This specifically targets customers who search specific brand-related keywords and who already know the presence of the brand. In doing so, more information about the brand is delivered to customers. It also increases awareness of the brand by encouraging those who search the brand to visit the official web page. Furthermore, Baidu Brand Zone's advertisement is effective in strengthening the brand's value. Figure 10 is the image of an actual Brand Zone of NIKE (Baidu.com, 2018).

Figure 10.   NIKE Brand Zone advertisement on Baidu (Baidu.com, 2018).

In conclusion, Baidu's marketing is aligned with the development of current target marketing. Baidu obtains a great advantage in aggregating the huge amounts of information gathered from Internet users on the database. This helps marketers create more customised and personalised advertisements based on individuals' unique demographics, search patterns and intentions.

WeChat

Internet censorship and SNS in China

China has a unique censorship environment that is different from the United States and South Korea. With the rapid growth of SNS, the Chinese government is restricting and suppressing information, content and comments on websites primarily to exercise political and social control over the population (Yanes and Berger, 2017). However, the Chinese government's strict regulations and control on Weibo rather boosted the spread of WeChat across China. Although censorship on WeChat posts still exists, only 1.5% of posts are coercively restricted by the government, and these are mainly due to certain technical aspects (Tu, 2016). Due to the closed WeChat's networking system, sensitive content can spread quickly and widely before it gets deleted by government authorities, while in the meantime people can still send sensitive messages through voice recording.

Therefore, WeChat attracts massive numbers of daily users through secure interaction and communication.

In such an environment where a number of foreign social media such as Instagram and Facebook are prohibited, the 'home-grown network' WeChat, created by Tencent, plays a significant role in integrating China's 1.3 billion population (Yanes and Berger, 2017). WeChat is the Chinese texting and voice messaging application with more than 900 million daily users (Li, 2018). As shown in Figure 11, about 25% of WeChat users access WeChat between 11 and 30 times every day (Yanes and Berger, 2017). With increasing usage and number of downloaders, WeChat is extending its services to payment, QR coding and channels for Brands to communicate.

It is common in China that people make payments using QR codes even on the street. WeChat as a social media platform now provides a payment service called WeChat Pay. It not only reduces the time it takes to pay for things, by eliminating cash payments but also gives discounts and promotions when using WeChat. Sellers often provide discount

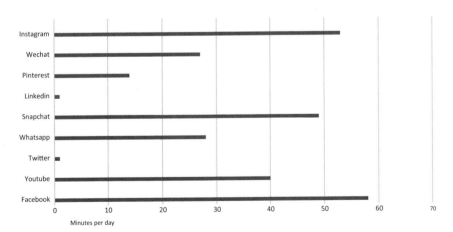

Figure 11.   Number of times per day that WeChat users in China access WeChat in March 2016 (Yanes and Berger, 2017).

vouchers to customers through WeChat, which ultimately improves the shopping experience.

> With regard to a total number of users, WeChat Pay still stands over Alipay getting a total of 806 million monthly active users as compared to Alipay's 450 million monthly users.
>
> When it comes to total market share though, Alipay still has the upper hand. Alipay still had 50.42% of the market share in 2016 while WeChat Pay had 38.12%. It's pretty interesting to note though that Alipay's market share dropped from 74.92% in 2015 to 50.42% in 2016. This was a 24.5% drop in one year!
>
> In contrast, WeChat's market share actually went up in 2016. From 11.43% in 2015, it reached 38.12% in 2016 which is a 26.69% increase! It seems like the trend is that the gap between the two is lessening and WeChat Pay may actually catch up to Alipay soon.[10]

Targeting strategies on WeChat

Tencent has the ability to segment target groups based on demographic characteristics, interests, keyword searching, behaviour and environment. Like Baidu's advertisements, WeChat understands customers' social interests, shopping intentions and online behaviour by integrating not only gender, location and age but also past online activities, networking histories and keyword searches (Li, 2018).

There are two main channels of advertising on WeChat, specifically *Moments advertising* and *Banner advertising* (Li, 2018).

WeChat Moments advertising

Moments advertising displays brands on moments (timeline) on WeChat. Moments advertisements show ads in advanced ways. Marketers can choose their target audience by choosing a location, past networks, demographics and device types. Specifically, marketers can choose among more than 30 cities or 42 different foreign countries according to not only

---

[10] *Source*: www.medium.com.

location category but also target age, gender, level of educational and marital status. In addition, the monitoring of individual user behaviour on WeChat is incorporated in the marketing strategy (Chen, 2018). If the customer shows interest in the ad by liking, commenting or clicking the link, the user is more likely to see similar ads next time. However, if the audience did not react to the advertisement in a timeline of six hours, the ad disappears and is replaced by another ad that better matches the audience's needs (Chen, 2018) (Figure 12).

WeChat Banner advertising

The WeChat banner advertisement is displayed at the very bottom of the page. This simply shows the brand name, logo and a call-to-action button. Banner advertising is less effective than Moment advertising, as marketers can only choose general targets such as based on certain demographics (Chen, 2018). In fact, advertisers doubt the effectiveness of banner advertising as audiences usually skip and do not click on the link. Still, banner advertising increases brand awareness by encouraging users to follow official brand websites, sign up for monthly news and download codes for coupons (Chen, 2018).

In conclusion, WeChat is an attractive platform for target marketing where users can actively interact and react to brands, even in China's

WeChat is considered a paramount <u>Chinese digital marketing channel</u> for international brands doing businesses in China. Especially WeChat Moments ads is a booming trend that brings more opportunities for marketers to advertise in China.

What is WeChat Moments Advertising?
Advertising on WeChat Moments is a similar method as advertising on Facebook allowing brands to place ads on their news feed. It gives users the feeling that their "friends" send an advertisement on their WeChat moments, but with an additional "Sponsored" tag in the upper right corner. WeChat Moments ads provides advertisers with high quality user data based on which marketers can define their target audience according to age, gender, location, industry etc.

Figure 12.   WeChat Moments advertisement (Dragon Social, 2018).

censorship environment. As Tencent is now providing a range of services on platforms other than WeChat, there is a growing number of advertising options for marketers in targeting different customer groups. Therefore, WeChat's advertising strategy also aligns with the current trend of target marketing, including target age, gender, level of educational and marital status. In addition, the monitoring of individual user behaviour on WeChat is incorporated in the marketing strategy (Chen, 2018). If the customer shows interest in the ad by liking, commenting or clicking the link, the user is more likely to see similar ads next time. However, if the audience did not react to the advertisement in a timeline of six hours, the ad disappears and is replaced with another ad that better matches the audience's needs (Chen, 2018).

Comparisons between the Two Countries

(1) *Keyword recognition*

It was found that the United States (Google) and China (Baidu) have good opportunities to make use of the current target marketing possibilities. While Google and Baidu are similar in understanding customer needs from keyword searches, Naver focused on the accuracy of keyword matching. One reason for the difference can be found in keyword recognition.

Specifically, Naver is strong at matching exact keywords. It offers keyword ideas from Autocomplete and Related Searches. By providing various keyword options, users can select and use the keywords that are most relevant to their search intentions. When carrying out a search using a keyword, Naver provides search results from knowledge iN, user blogs and Naver's social community, named Café. Figure 13 illustrates an example of search results. The contents created by Naver users are displayed on the top, and other related websites are displayed at the bottom.

In contrast, Google offers a few related keywords. Users are not able to explore keyword ideas from the list of keywords. Google, however, as well as Baidu both understand users' intentions; and so once a keyword search is made, they provide more detailed and specific information based on the user usage behaviour. Modern machine learning techniques will be used to understand customer behaviour better as illustrated in Figures 13 and 14.

(2) *Data usage rates*

Data analysis capabilities are essential in current target marketing. Both the United States and China are putting lots of effort into Big Data and R&D to effectively utilise customer data. However, the data usage rate was significantly low in South Korea compared to the other two countries. The current data usage status and reasons for the low data usage rates in South Korea will therefore be further explored to determine which actions should be taken to grow in accordance with the current target marketing strategies.

According to the results of the latest survey conducted by Korea Information Science Promotion Agency (NIA), the utilisation of Big Data, infrastructures and systems in South Korea is below expectations (Choi, 2016). Consequently, SNS and search engines in South Korea

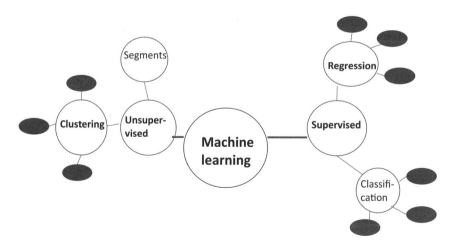

Figure 13.   Structure of the machine learning.

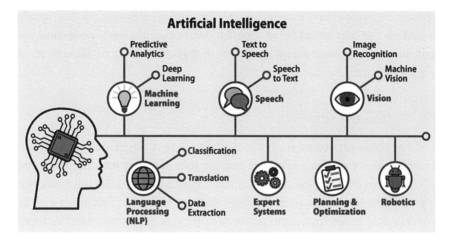

Figure 14.   Structure of artificial intelligence.

are not prepared to contact customers with the data on a customer-specific basis.

There are some obstacles to introducing the data analysis system in South Korea. Firstly, there is no data yet that could be called Big Data. Most companies do not have the experience to move on to advanced Big Data analysis. Moreover, South Korean companies are not fully aware of the impact of Big Data analysis, which is why CEOs and CIOs are indifferent to Big Data analysis. In addition, the lack of a data-driven decision-making culture in the business environment is a major obstacle. This is because while search engines and SNS in both the United States and China encompass an enormous number of users on a global scale, Naver and Kakao are mostly locally based.

It is worth mentioning that there is a lack of understanding regarding what Big Data Analysis and Big Data itself can achieve. Most companies do not know how to use Big Data because there are only a few companies that use Big Data analysis, so South Korean companies are not yet ready to use it effectively.

Big Data analysis to leap one step further and cope with the era of the Fourth Industrial Revolution. Using Big Data will help domestic companies to get a total view of customers and sell products to the right customers, which will also help them to respond quickly to changing patterns of demand. Figure 15 presents the reasons for not introducing Big Data Analysis.

The lack of experts and the small open ecosystem also hinder the introduction and use of Big Data compared to nations overseas such as the United States and China.

On the other hand, due to the increasing number of cases related to the disclosure of personal customer information, customers in South Korea have a strong negative view of data sharing and use. Since the advent of the Internet era, customers have struggled with personal data loss, and the introduction of Big Data in South Korea has been hampered by stricter government regulations.

The lack of data is the main reason for the inability to use Big Data analysis in South Korea. It is expected that the situation will gradually improve as the goal of the Internet of Things (IoT) application gradually expands (Choi, 2016). However, customers' perceptions on data collection are still negative due to privacy issues. These perceptions should be changed through government policy in order to implement Big Data analysis. South Korea should tackle the fundamental cause of concerns regarding collecting personal data by strengthening the security system.

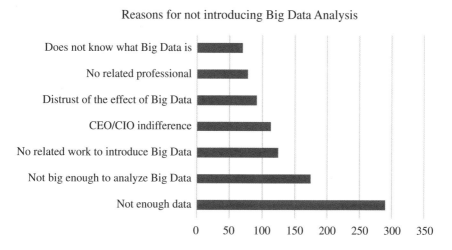

Figure 15. Reasons for not introducing Big Data Analysis in South Korea (Choi, 2016).

Thereafter, successful cases and application models with Big Data analysis to which companies can refer should be provided in order to encourage the collection and use of Big Data.

In summary, South Korean companies and governments should make efforts to revive.

Conclusions

Search engines and social networking services in both the United States and China share similar aspects of target marketing which are characterised by the use of Big Data and algorithms. Naver and KakaoTalk, also offer services based on big data analysis by using a big data platform for target marketing. Despite differences between the countries in the way they carry out target marketing, they certainly reflect each countries' different but unique characteristics: the US's dominant position in the social media industry, Korea's local-based social media network, and China's Internet censorship environment.

Although target marketing raises privacy concerns regarding the use of personal data (Davies, 2017), customers do, in fact, enjoy benefits from target marketing. These include personalised offers and recommendations analysed from previous shopping patterns and individual shopping intentions (Davies, 2017). Younger generations actively utilise SNS to get purchase information and recognise the benefits of target marketing in the hope of improving their shopping experience (Davies, 2017). With a massive amount of available data, target marketing is expected to become more identity-based, automated and therefore, practical.

In the near future, computers and artificial intelligence may be able to infer users' psychological traits and react accordingly. Marketers would then be capable of more accurately matching ads to an individual customer's personality. What is more, products and services could adjust automatically to best match users' character traits and alterations in moods through machine learning (*The Guardian*, 2015). Finally, the effects of data leverage with technology advancements are enormous, which is why so many social media users, marketers and platforms expected such a promising future.

Bibliography

Baidu Advertising (2018). *Guide to Baidu's PPC Interface.* Available at: https://www. baiduadvertising.com/baidu-ppc-interface-guide/#matchtype (Accessed 25 October 2018).

Baidu press releases (2016). *Baidu Announces Fourth Quarter and Fiscal Year 2016 Results.* Available at: http://ir.baidu.com/phoenix.zhtml?c=188488&p=irol-newsArticle&ID=2248999 (Accessed 25 October 2018).

Baidu.com (2018a). *nike_百度搜索.* Available at: https://www.baidu.com/s?ie= utf-8&f=8&rsv_bp=0&rsv_idx=1&tn=baidu&wd=nike&rsv_pq=b2c12928 000055b0&rsv_t=ed01tmSBuxDVvr5N6RLUBrIM0fNhqjwKOCCZOcdPmHG MY46GSwe3yuR1Pm0&rqlang=cn&rsv_enter=1&rsv_sug3=4&rsv_sug2= 0&inputT=635&rsv_sug4=63 5 (Accessed 25 October 2018).

baidu.com (2018b). *Search Services.* Available at: http://ir.baidu.com/phoenix. zhtml?c=188488&p=irol-searchservices (Accessed 25 October 2018).

Cahill, D. (1997). Target Marketing and Segmentation: Valid and Useful Tools for Marketing. *Management Decision*, 35(1), pp. 10–13.

Chard, T. (n.d.). Facebook Advertising for Ecommerce Entrepreneurs. [ebook] pp. 17–30. Available at: https://www.shopify.com/guides/facebook-advertising/ types (Accessed 22 October 2018).

Chen, T. (2018). *Advertising on WeChat: A Step by Step Guide — WalktheChat.* WalktheChat. Available at: https://walkthechat.com/advertising-on-wechat-moment/ (Accessed 26 October 2018).

China Whisper (2018). *Top 5 Chinese Search Engine in 2017.* Available at: http:// www.chinawhisper.com/top-5-chinese-search-engine-in-2017/ (Accessed 25 October 2018).

Chiu, C., Guild, T., and Orr, G. (2015). *Five Keys to Connecting with China's Wired Consumers,* McKinsey Digital, McKinsey & Company, pp. 1–5.

Chiu, C., Ip, C., and Silverman, A. (2012). *Understanding Social Media in China,* Marketing & Sales practice. McKinsey & Company, pp. 1–4.

Choi, J. (2016). Status of Big Data Analysis and its Implications. *KISTEP InI*, 14, pp. 33–43.

Davies, J. (2017). *Consumers Like Targeted Marketing Despite Privacy Concerns.* Available at: http://digitalmarketingmagazine.co.uk/digital-marketing-data/ consumers-like-targeted-marketing-despite-privacy-concerns/4531 (Accessed 25 October 2018).

Dragon Social (2018). *WeChat Advertising 101: All You Need to Know.* Available at: https://www.dragonsocial.net/blog/wechat-advertising/ (Accessed 26 October 2018).

Emarketer.com (2017). *KakaoTalk Users and Penetration in South Korea, 2016–2021 (millions, % of Mobile Phone Messaging Users and % of Smartphone Users) — eMarketer.* [online] Available at: https://www.emarketer.com/Chart/KakaoTalkUsers-Penetration-South-Korea-2016-2021-millions-of-mobile-phone-messagingusers-of-smartphone-users/209378 (Accessed 23 October 2018).

Han, J. and Cho, O. (2015). Platform business eco-model evolution: Case study on KakaoTalk in Korea. *Journal of Open Innovation: Technology, Market, and Complexity*, 1(6).

Hinchcliffe (2017). The rise of the 4th platform: Pervasive Communitydata devices and intelligence, May 4 2015.

Jang, Y. and Youn, W. (2014). A study on promotional plans of local business by using SNS (Social Network Service): Focused on Naver band, Blog, KakaoTalk and Facebook. *Journal of Economics, Marketing and Management*, 2(2), pp. 1–9.

Johnson, A. (2017). *Sprinklr Spotlight: KakaoTalk & KakaoStory — Sprinklr.* Sprinklr. Available at: https://blog.sprinklr.com/sprinklr-spotlight-kakaotalk-kakaostory/ (Accessed 22 October 2018).

Kazım Kirtiş, A. and Karahan, F. (2011). To be or not to be in social media arena as the most cost-efficient marketing strategy after the global recession. *Procedia — Social and Behavioral Sciences*, 24, pp. 260–268.

Krush, A. (n.d.). *Google Vs. Naver: Why Can't Google Dominate Search in Korea? | SEO Blog of Link Assistant.Com.* Link-assistant.com. Available at: https://www.link assistant.com/blog/google-vs-naver-why-cant-google-dominatesearch-in-korea/ (Accessed 22 October 2018).

Lee, J. (2015). Consumers and targeted marketing in the digital age. *Oricom Brand Journal*, 71, pp. 1–3.

Lee, M. (2018). *Naver Keyword Tool Explained: The Keyword Planner for Korea.* Available at: http://www.theegg.com/seo/korea/naver-keyword-tool explained (Accessed 22 October 2018).

Li, S. (2018). *The New Guide to WeChat Advertising*, Sheng Li Digital, pp. 1–35.

Lua, A. (2017). The Complete Guide to Instagram Ads: A Step-by-Step Guide to Advertising on Instagram. [Blog] Social Blog. Available at: https://blog.buff-erapp.com/instagram-ads-guide# (Accessed 22 October 2018).

Lynn, M. (2011). *Segmenting and Targeting Your Market: Strategies and Limitations.* Cornell University, School of Hospitality Administration. Available at: https://pdfs.semanticscholar.org/c736/f493cf24b9414dcc47c6862f9875ce8537f5.pdf (Accessed 23 October 2018).

Mangold, W. and Faulds, D. (2009). Social media: The new hybrid element of the promotion mix. *Business Horizons*, 52(4), pp. 357–365.

Marketing China (2018). *Baidu Advertising — Marketing China*. Available at: https://www.marketingtochina.com/baidu-advertising/ (Accessed 25 October 2018).

Medium (2017). *What Is Kakao and Why Should You Care? — Alive Studios — Medium*. Available at: https://medium.com/@madebyalive/what-is-kakao-and- whyshould-you-carefcb430bc61d0 (Accessed 22 October 2018).

Ok, H. (2011). New media practices in Korea. *International Journal of Communication*, 5, pp. 320–348.

Osterwalder, A. and Pigneur Y. (2010). *Business Model Generation: A Handbook for Visionaries, Game Changers, and Challengers*, Wiley.

Panjala, N. (2018). *South Korean Business Environment and Startup Ecosystem*. Theseus.fi. Available at: https://www.theseus.fi/bitstream/handle/10024/ 149259/Thesis%20Nina%20Pajala.pf? sequence 1 (Accessed 22 October 2018).

Saedu.naver.com (2018). *Naver Advertisements*. Available at: https://saedu. naver.com/adbiz/searchad/clickChoiceProduct.nhn (Accessed 23 October 2018).

Sampi. (2018). *How to Get the Most Out of Your Marketing in China?* Available at: https://sampi.co/advertising-on-baidu-most-comprehensive-overview/ (Accessed 25 October 2018).

Statista (2018a). *Global Social Media Ranking 2018 | Statistic*. Available at: https:// www.statista.com/statistics/272014/global-social-networks-ranked-by-number-of-users/ (Accessed 22 October 2018).

Statista (2018b). *Kakaotalk: Number of Monthly Active Users Worldwide 2018 | Statistic*. Available at: https://www.statista.com/statistics/278846/kakaotalk-monthlyactive- users-mau/ (Accessed 22 October 2018).

Studio98 (2017). *How Google Is Changing Target Marketing Strategies*. Available at: https://www.studio98.com/google-changing-target-marketing-strategies (Accessed 23 October 2018).

Support.google.com (2018). *About Google Ads Campaign Types — Previous — Google Partners Help*. Available at: https://support.google.com/partners/ answer/2567043?co=ADWORDS.IsAWNCustomer%3Dfalse&hl=en (Accessed 22 October 2018).

Support.google.com (2018). *Targeting Your Ads — Google Ads Help*. Available at: https://support.google.com/google-ads/answer/1704368 (Accessed 22 October 2018).

Suttle, R. (n.d.). *The Disadvantages of Target Marketing*. Smallbusiness.chron. com. Available at: https://smallbusiness.chron.com/disadvantages-target-marketing-36131.html (Accessed 23 October 2018).

The Guardian (2015). *Your Computer Knows You Better than your Friends Do, Say Researchers*. [online] Available at: https://www.theguardian.com/ technology/2015/jan/13/your-computer-knows-you-researchers-cambridge-stanford-university (Accessed 25 October 2018).

Tu, F. (2016). WeChat and Civil Society in China. *Communication and the Public*, 1(3), pp. 343–350.

Whatley, H. (2013). Chinese Internet Companies and Their Quest for Globalization. *SSRN Electronic Journal*, pp. 229–235.

Wordstream.com (2018a). *Online Ads: A Guide to Online Ad Types and Formats*. Available at: https://www.wordstream.com/online-ads#Google%20Search%20 Ads (Accessed 22 October 2018).

Wordstream.com (2018b). *Search Engine Marketing (SEM): What It Is & How to Do It Right | WordStream*. Available at: https://www.wordstream.com/search-engine-marketing (Accessed 22 October 2018).

Yoon, A. (2017). Role of communication in data reuse, *Asis&T*, 54(1), pp. 463–471.

Yoon, H. (2017). *Preferred SNS is Different in All Age Groups ... Target marketing, consideration of channel is fundamental*. [online] Biz.chosun.com. Available at: http://biz.chosun.com/site/data/html_dir/2017/02/08/2017020802074. html (Accessed 22 October 2018).

Yanes, P. A. and Berger, P. D. (2017). How WeChat has changed the face of marketing in China, *British Journal of Marketing Studies*, 5(3), pp. 14–21.

Chapter 10

Towards the Future: Join In or Disappear?

The traditional developments are the pillars for the future. As we see in the platform evolution, this third phase forms the prelude for the fourth phase. This fourth phase involves the connected world, whereby networks lie at the heart of our lives and how we do business. Connectivity is important, as is support at every desired (or undesired) moment. Location-based services, smart devices and communication data lie at the very foundation of this network structure and the application of new smart technology. As the Internet is used, it is possible to record all contacts and activities. This allows both active and passive links to be made: active, if a connection is made on the basis of triggers, alerts and pre-programmed connections; and passive, if the activities are recorded and the analysis lead to new activities on the basis of this; or if the user actively uses the function himself or wishes to acquire information, alongside proactive messages. This can be seen if, for example, on the basis of location-based services (and algorithms) you automatically receive traffic information (also if you are cycling) or if you automatically get route suggestions when you are regularly travelling a particular route. Traffic jam information and travel delays are taken into account here. You can also be automatically informed in shopping centres regarding special offers, activities or available parking spaces (Figure 1).

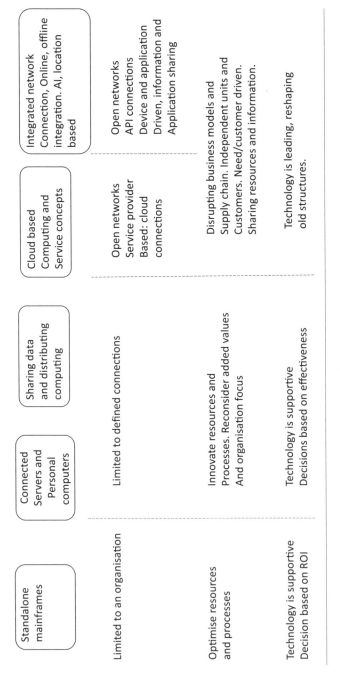

Figure 1.   Evolution of technology and impact on resources.

The future competition will be strongly determined by the application of the following:

- technology at business partners (externally-oriented applications);
- algorithms, which will guide and stimulate future behaviour;
- collaboration based on networking organisation;
- bonding and adoption by customers (a competitive advantage is created through a strong bond with customers);
- new business models (not based on cost price, but on value exchange).

Technology

The fourth phase of platforms and network connections will lead to a close relationship between individual clusters, companies, data files, personal details and location data. This involves, for example, Apple's home concept or Google's connected concept (Nest) connecting home devices. Devices, such as heating, lights or domestic equipment, can be activated remotely. Google Nest is a similar concept, whereby the thermostat, front door and cameras can be linked to one another. This fourth phase of *connecting computing*, where devices are interconnected, is *the Internet of things* (IoT). A network forms the basis of all the developments. It is important to be part of this network, whereby the cloud offers the facilities to use the software or services it has available, wherever you are. This connectivity can be far-reaching, as in theory there is no longer any limitation to connecting equipment and devices. The development and use of the 5G network will have a considerable influence on this development. This application will influence every facet of business and the lives of private individuals, a number of which are described as follows:

- Smart homes with all sorts of equipment that are connected and can automatically activate and deactivate one another. These may involve manual connections, usually by using apps or a smartphone. Or, they may involve physical triggers, such as an intruder alert, or lights or music switching on when you get home, or the microwave being activated. Concepts such as Google home and Alexa can help to support this further.

- New developments in the area of transport. We already see that with self-driving cars, and also with transport on demand where separate components of transport are linked to one another, for example train to taxi, and car to car park and train. In commercial transport, track and trace can be linked to delivery alerts or signals sent to the right loading bay so that cargo can be prepared or made ready for delivery. Empty lorries can automatically send a signal to a cargo database to see whether a new cargo is ready to be loaded. Connecting separate modes of transport through the Internet to particular functions is actually nothing new. This may form the basis for road user charging, but is currently already the basis for the registration of business mileage in a passenger car in relation to car fleet management or fiscal exemptions (fiscal addition).
- Safety and security applications that are linked to video recording (such as with Google's Nest concept), physical alert functions where an alert is linked to security services.
- Also in manufacturing processes, IoT and networks will form the basis for other production methods such as production on demand. Delivery for complex projects (project management) or customised products by linking user wishes to machines, for example, based on configurators.
- There are also well-known applications in the agricultural and environmental sectors where control is linked to external conditions. Examples include sowing and harvesting according to the weather and other links in the network, energy linked to the ambient temperature, as well as office temperature and lighting adjusted according to the number of people present in the building or room. Alternative energy sources and support energy sources are also linked to one another in a network based on algorithms.
- The applications in the healthcare sector are still in their early stages. Healthcare is a complex sector with many dominant players, from medical specialists in independent organisations, to hospitals (usually a cluster of organisations), insurance companies, pharmaceutical companies and the government. This involves a complex of mutual agreements, legislation and interests that are not easy to fit into a platform approach. It requires another look at healthcare, a different role for the

patient and the hospital (physical service) and a different 'balance of power'. Due to the many opposing forces of all the interested parties, it is currently difficult to implement changes on the basis of value exchange and efficiency. It is possible, however, that the sharply rising costs may form the trigger for change. In any case, the technology and networks are ready for this.

- The physical world, our immediate environment, is also interconnected; smart cities that respond to environmental effects, accessibility, traffic intensity, lighting and parking. A complex of independent elements from our personal living environments are interconnected via sensors, so that more service can be created for the residents and visitors, as well as greater efficiency (lower costs) in, for example, energy consumption.

- And finally: the ultimate contact point between consumers, businesses and (web)shops. Particularly, the change in supply and the application of the Internet and networks are leading to a different behaviour. The Internet offers many advantages for the consumer, such as home deliveries, 24/7 support and an unlimited choice of products and services. All applications can be interconnected, as described in the section regarding multisided platforms. This has led to major disruptions in the retail sector, based on customer preferences. The challenge for physical shops lies in motivating customers once more to go to the shops and buy there. This requires a more detailed analysis of the buying behaviour and buying motives. A clear focus on the value that one can add, with a link to a form of collaboration in the supply chain, is also essential in order to survive. The exact same preconditions and principles apply here as I have already described.

It is clear that competitive relationships will undergo a thorough change.

Half of the 4500 hosting companies and cloud hosting companies are under threat

The Dutch IT sector is facing a major depletion. Within five years, half of the 4500 hosting companies and cloud hosting companies will no longer exist in the traditional form.

This is the prediction made by Rabobank in its most recent market analysis of IT services.

Researchers of the bank suggest that the expected restructuring of the market power of major international technology companies, particularly Amazon Web Services (AWS) and Microsoft, are the reason. The rapidly changing technology will also play a role. 'AWS and Microsoft are forcing hosting parties in the Netherlands to make strategic choices. The financial capacity in combination with the rapid rate of technological developments is for many smaller providers in this market simply impossible to keep up with,' suggest the Rabo researchers.

They point out that smaller IT companies that offer fairly generic hosting services will in the long term run the risk of being squeezed out of the market. 'Larger parties are cheaper, more flexible and more innovative.' These larger IT providers are currently busy with takeovers, often supported by private equity, in order to create economies of sale or to claim a position in the top of the (international) market.[1]

The potency of the changes depends on the strength and the participants in the network. This is illustrated in Figure 2.

The application of IoT and artificial intelligence (AI) within this value chain will lead to the customer experience becoming more personal and responding better and at the right time through interaction and communication. The basis of marketing will change from

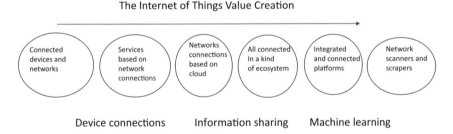

Figure 2.   Value chain of IoT.

---

[1] *Source*: https://fd.nl/ondernemen/1273525/helft-van-4500-cloud-en-hostingbedrijven-dreigt-te-verdwijnen.

transaction-based to value-based, the exchange of values. In addition to the product or services, the extra dimension of personal contact can be initiated individually. IoT and AI will be leading components in this value exchange. This is a great challenge for organisations. Within the digital transformation in the value chain and the business model, IoT and AI must play a leading role as part of a personal experience. As an organisation falls short here due to its history, hierarchical structure and sales focus, the collaboration within the network (value chain) is essential. Real-time connections, communication and analysis of needs are essential. This applies for every value chain, whether aimed at consumers, businesses or the industrial market. The competition will on the basis of these values be different than in the past, as has already been described.

- Technology forms the basis for communication, IoT and AI.
- Data is analysed on the basis of historical behaviour and expected future behaviour.
- Knowledge is translated into algorithms.
- Networks determine the competitive strength in markets.
- Companies determine the competitive strength within the platform and the network.

The automation tools, too, have to meet the requirements of the network economy and the subsequent constraints. The chapter on technology examined the requirements for quick connections, speedy modifications and the sharing of information and data within both an organisation and the network. The traditional systems focus on the traditional forms of organisations and the required information provision from a supply-driven perspective. New possibilities, however, are making it possible to quickly add or modify functions. The link with external systems is made through a separate application for each system to be connected, so-called APIs, which can be programmed as independent applications. The functions and the information provision can be divided into microservice units, thereby allowing a specific application to be programmed. By linking the microservices, algorithms are created that support the operations and the business model (Figure 3).

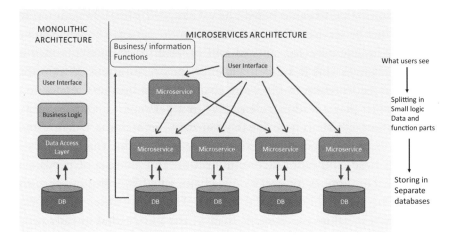

Figure 3.   Microservices set-up.

Source: Based on algoritmia.com

Artificial Intelligence[2]

AI is a very promising area of technology that is being developed in many sectors, and the retail and manufacturing sectors are no exception to this. AI is still not sufficiently developed to assess what precisely its impact will be. Combined with IoT, a transparency is created; also, the combination of data can ensure that automatic modifications can be made to the user interface, the information provision and the algorithm. This will make it possible to precisely guide both the customer behaviour and the production capacity. Also, in combination with a platform's selection and matching module, it is possible to offer a more suitable range of products and services along with the associated prices. An example is dynamic pricing, where the price depends on the demand (Ryanair and Uber) or the time or period, with lower prices in the evening or last-minute deals. The application of AI currently involves the analysis of a large database with vast amounts of relevant data. Based on predictive modelling, algorithms are made for communication and promotions.

---

[2] Partly based on the research of RSM/Erasmus University students Kristel Tan, Lum Shun, Yi Richelle and Pim Fijt.

Thanks to the analyses, tasks can be carried out more effectively without any explicit programming being required. In addition to the more obvious increased efficiency in the area of logistics and production, there are also advantages to be gained in the application of AI in contacts with the customer, particularly through a platform or network. An example of this is Watson, which can search for connections in large information databases and make a suggestion based on these. IBM's Watson is already being used to a limited degree in the healthcare sector for analysing clinical symptoms and interpreting the possible underlying pathologies. The same technology is being used by The North Face in its sales. Customers are helped to find products that best suit their personal preferences. The results appear to be positive, as the technology has contributed to generating a click frequency of 60% for product recommendations and has generally led to positive feedback (Fry, 2018).[3]

The back-end applications of AI are also interesting; perhaps even more interesting considering the developments of the network economy. This can be seen in, for example, the production processes where robotics is used. Fanuc, a Japanese company specialised in AI and robotics, has an AI called Gakushu Learning Software that is integrated in robots in order to collect data via sensors, which can then be used for controlling the robot. One company that uses this technology is Tesla. Tesla's traditional production efficiency is perhaps not yet optimal, but once AI technology has been refined even further the use of robots with AI will bring about a revolution in the way products are made. Also, in the contacts with customers it will be possible to better adapt the supply to the demand. In addition, combined with printing on demand, the strength of the network will grow even further.

Collaboration Leads to Strength and Knowledge

This new network infrastructure is based on new system possibilities such as cloud applications, software containers and microservices. But within

---

[3] Refer also to Fry, Hannah (2018). *Hello World*, Penguin Random House, London, p. 79 ff.

the collaboration, quality control and reliability are also of utmost importance. In the old supply chain, it was clear what the accountability was of each link and each independent entity. In a network, there is a joint accountability and joint quality control. Reliability has to be part of the entire network. It is on the basis of this need that new applications have been developed, blockchain being the most well known.

The 'blocks' in the blockchain consist of digital pieces of information. They have in fact three applications:

- Blocks store information on transactions, for example, the dates, time and the amount in the currency of the most recent purchase.
- Blocks store information on the parties participating in transactions. Instead of using the buyer's real name, the purchase is registered without any identifying information by means of a unique 'digital signature', comparable to a user name.
- Blocks store information that distinguishes them from other blocks. Each block has a unique code, called a hash, thereby distinguishing them from other blocks.

In this way, the actions within a network can be recorded without it being possible to change them. This results in the activities on the platforms and the involvement in transactions and activities being regarded as highly reliable (Figure 4).

The Road to the Future is a Gradual Process

The model in Figure 5 describes the developments in the following two phases:

- The adaptation of the traditional model based on digital applications, *doing digital.* This leads to efficiency, but is not sufficient for competitive strength in the future. In this first phase, companies apply automation along with providing online service. The possibilities of a new digital channel are also considered, the so-called multichannel strategy. As described previously, a multichannel strategy does not lead to disruption or any extra-competitive strength. The attention has to be

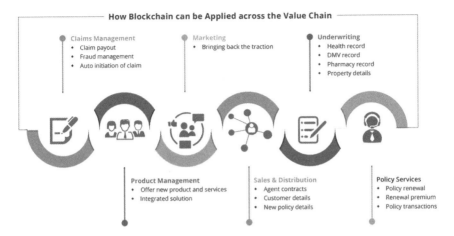

Figure 4.   Blockchain and the value chain (2018).[5]

divided over two channels, each with their own rules, strengths and weaknesses. This is practically impossible in a traditional organisation. For this reason, there is always one channel that is leading and one channel that provides support. Traditional organisations are based on physical possibilities and automation applications based on traditional structures. They tend not to focus on a new digital channel as much as they do on the traditional channel, which they know inside out. The supporting digital channel will mainly be used to provide information and service. Traditional automation systems (monolith) will restrict the change/transformation of the business model.

- The second phase of adapting the organisation to make it future proof is based on the digital possibilities of the network economy (being digital). These organisations fit within a form of collaboration, whereby the unity of the collaboration determines the competitive strength. The added value is jointly determined, as is the supply for buyers on the basis of value exchange. This also marks the transformation from a supply-oriented economy to an economy based on demand. This transformation is only possible by putting data and collaboration at the core

[4] https://www.kisspng.com/png-life-insurance-blockchain-value-chain-block-chain-5001274/preview.html.

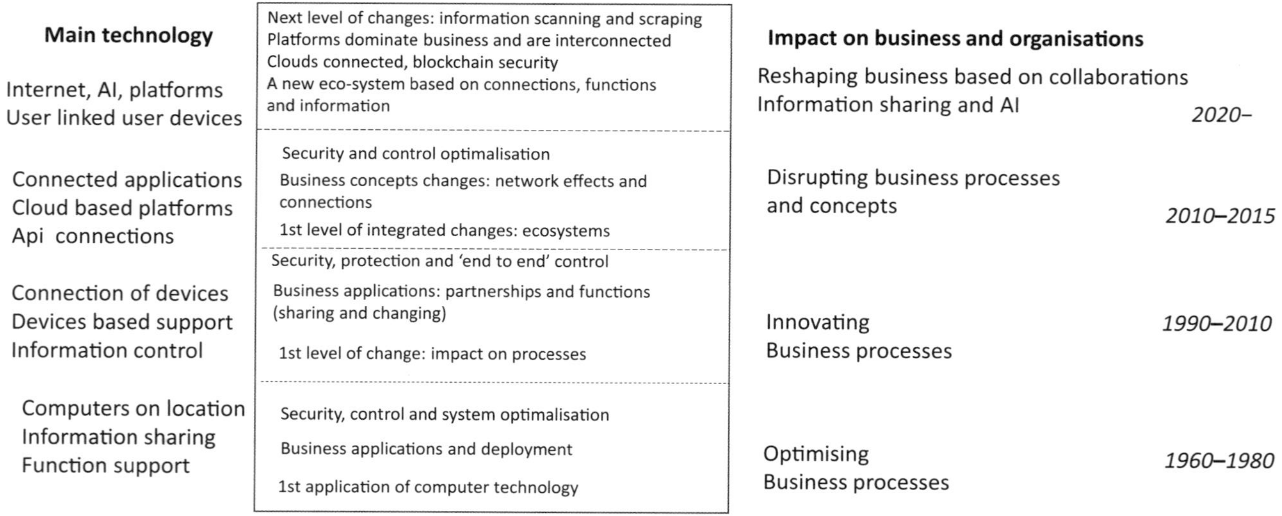

Main technology		Impact on business and organisations	
Internet, AI, platforms User linked user devices	Next level of changes: information scanning and scraping Platforms dominate business and are interconnected Clouds connected, blockchain security A new eco-system based on connections, functions and information	Reshaping business based on collaborations Information sharing and AI	2020–
Connected applications Cloud based platforms Api connections	Security and control optimalisation Business concepts changes: network effects and connections 1st level of integrated changes: ecosystems	Disrupting business processes and concepts	2010–2015
Connection of devices Devices based support Information control	Security, protection and 'end to end' control Business applications: partnerships and functions (sharing and changing) 1st level of change: impact on processes	Innovating Business processes	1990–2010
Computers on location Information sharing Function support	Security, control and system optimalisation Business applications and deployment 1st application of computer technology	Optimising Business processes	1960–1980

Figure 5. Development of digital strategies.

of an organisation's activities. The data is shared by all parties in the network. Based on this data, not only are the digital possibilities applied but direct communication also takes place within the network with customers and with all relevant parties.

The strength of this sharing of information, joint application of data and strategy based on analyses and communication is such that the independent providers in the supply economy no longer have sufficient competitive strength to survive on their own. As a result, they will either become a niche player or join a network.

As can be seen from Figure 5, the technology crucial for the coming years is now already available. It is the adoption of these digital possibilities within new preconditions and frameworks that make a change in the business model necessary. Many companies are currently struggling with this transformation. Governments need to align the necessary legislation. The flexible deployment of freelancers and the profit circumvention of global platforms are currently issues of particular concern for which the traditional legislation and regulations do not yet have an answer. The developments described not only determine the competitive strength of organisations but also require a modification to the ecosystem, the environment. Companies that stubbornly cling onto the old environment or old rules at a national or regional level will fall by the wayside. The developments of Uber versus traditional taxi companies and webshops versus the limitations of physical shops (location, for example) are examples of this. The fact that this erodes the competitive strength for the future (and therefore leads to a decreased level of employment) is overlooked due to the short-term vision.

Necessary Changes for the Future

Organisations will have to adapt to the possibilities offered by technology (being digital), as well as to the wishes of customers (also companies), and furthermore to partnerships in the network and in particular to the fact that the collaboration leads to a loss of autonomy and control. All these aspects have an impact on the business model, leadership and all other business functions. The following three important areas can be identified here:

1. The customer and the customer's wishes and experiences: As I have described earlier, these form the basis for the demand-driven economy and are not the endpoint of a selling process. Based on the customer's wishes, not only must the organisation be flexible but the staff also need technical support and receive the relevant competencies and responsibilities.
2. This requires the flat organisation as described earlier: Flat means that it is possible to respond quickly and to have responsibility in all the relevant functions that are related to customers.
3. A third adaptation is the relationship within the network: The relationship between other (service) providers, the connection with information and knowledge networks and relevant data from the search and buying process.

These three layers are already present in organisations, but in reverse. From a production unit or function, the supporting functions are managed and then finally the market-oriented functions. The external communication is to a large degree product-driven. If there is interaction with the buyer, this generally involves selling motives or customer complaints. The organisation is top-down, hierarchically organised, and the flow of information is also from the top-down. This provides few opportunities for interaction or discussion. 'This is what the boss wants'. But now it is all about what a customer wants, to adapt the organisation and its culture according to the motto of 'customer first'. Information flows have to be guided from the outside to within. Those who have contact with customers, from the call centre to the salespeople, must be heard by the organisation and involved in the decision-making. For many organisations, managers and board members, this is a bridge too far with all the ensuing consequences (Figure 6).

Surviving in the Future?

- In the future, networks will be a pivotal factor. Networks within which all parties, production, customers, service providers and employees are connected via IoT and platforms (see Figure 7). Multisided platforms will gain ever more knowledge through data, sensors, AI and process

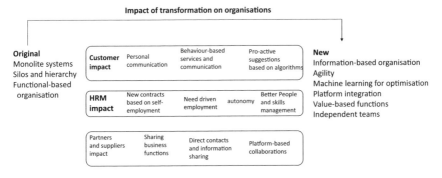

Figure 6.   Transforming an organisation.

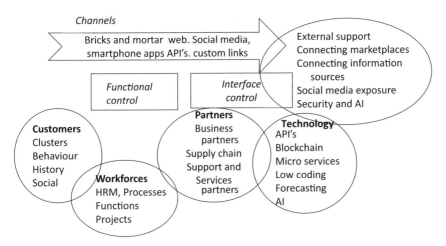

Figure 7.   Clusters are connected to one another through networks. Each cluster has its own competency of which all relevant parties form part.

analyses. This data is analysed 24/7 and will lead to a higher quality of products, matching and customer contact. Market structures will change, with organisations having to focus on competencies in order to be relevant for networks. In addition to large networks, there will also be space for niche players, provided they have a distinctive supply, special competencies and close customer contacts.

- The technological developments will be part of these networks and contribute to the quality of the contacts such as AI, IoT and real-time analyses. The technology is used in products for quality improvements and trust (blockchain). It comes down to acquiring a clear position within these developments. Organisations need to bond with customers; customer behaviour forms the basis for the future. This is what new revenue models will be based on, no longer on cost price or transactions.

- Developments can no longer be isolated into particular applications but will affect everyone precisely as described; the Fourth Industrial Revolution. Boundaries are fading, *geofencing* can only be used to a limited degree and competition can take place in all sorts of ways. But particularly in these current times of transformation and change it is all to do with the adoption and adaption of new possibilities. If structures, systems and the behaviour are not modified, then the technology will only support old activities and habits. However, if others (particularly customers) change their behaviour, you surely do not want to be left behind.

- Business models are changing into networks based on individual competencies. Companies work together on the basis of complementary skills. Networks are competing against one another, while companies within a network may also compete. The competition on the free market becomes a field of niche companies that have a specific added value with respect to the network. Revenue models are no longer based on margins alone, but are much more diverse whereby various sources of income are based on added value, services, associated services and collaborations.

- The pricing in platform business models is no longer based on a product's sales margin that can be increased through internal optimisation or differentiation of the product in order to justify a higher sales price. Price strategies for platforms have to determine part of the created value in order to generate income for the platform owner, and also have to improve the general value proposition of the platform. In view of the fact that price changes have direct consequences for the participants of the platform on both sides, pricing can only be deployed as a holistic measure (Reillier and Reillier, 2017). A decision to increase the price for producers can, for example, lead to a reduction of stocks, which in turn can result in less choice for consumers who may then be tempted to leave the platform. This would make the platform less attractive for other producers (and/or advertisers). In the literature, this is described as a negative network effect. Each customer segment produces a different flow of income. Platforms usually do not apply costs or lower prices for consumers that are subsidised by revenues from other customer segments (Osterwalder and Pigneur, 2010).

- The technology (particularly algorithms) will form the foundation for interaction, communication and customer bonding. Data will both lead to more knowledge regarding what is happening now as well as help to set out the path for what still needs to be done. There is no future without data. Speed of action (agility), flat, and mean and lean organisations are necessary.

- It is important to have courage, to respond and to learn. Even if you make mistakes, because these are useful learning experiences (Table 1).

Table 1.   The end of competition or simply a change in competition?

Basic Competitive Advantage	Do the Same, Only Better	Adapt Your Proposition	Future Competitive Advantage
Activities	Do the same as the competition, but better.	Do different things than your competition.	Ensure you have a distinctive proposition (same day delivery, right of return, customer service, algorithms, customer bonding).
Value creation	Satisfy the same needs, but at lower costs.	Satisfy other needs, or the same needs but at lower prices. Let the needs of your customer group guide you.	Part of a network/platform. Excel in the core elements of the needs (matching).
Advantage	Lower costs, but difficult to achieve.	Ensure that higher prices are accepted or realise lower costs.	Collaboration in a network, sharing of costs within the network (marketing costs), diversified business models.
Competition	Be the best and set yourself apart in the execution.	Ensure that you are unique and compete at a strategic level.	Respond better to customer wishes, be proactive. Be active at the decisive moment of the purchase. Bond and motivate your customers and use algorithms. Be part of a network.

Bibliography

Hinchcliffe, D. (2015). *The Rise of the 4th Platform: Pervasive Community, Data, Devices, and Intelligence,* On Digital Strategy, May 4 2015.

Osterwalder, A. and Pigneur, Y. (2010). *Business Model Generation: A Handbook for Visionaries, Game Changers, and Challengers,* Wiley.

Reillier, L. C. and Reillier, B. (2017). *Platform Strategy: How to Unlock the Power of Communities and Networks to Grow Your Business,* 1st edition, Routledge, p. 222.

Appendix 1

Bidfood: Development and Platform Strategy Rollout

Bidfood is an international food service business with operations in 36 countries and a turnover of €750 million in its Dutch operation. In the Netherlands, its most important customers are chefs, restaurant and hotel owners and the healthcare and catering market.

For 10 years now Bidfood Netherlands has been working on the development and rollout of its digital strategy. This can be roughly divided into the following four phases:

Phase 1: Digitalisation of Customer and Supplier

Bidfood started the rollout of its online strategy in 2010. From the very beginning the set-up was based on a platform strategy. This means that both the customer and the provider were included in the digitalisation. But what did this involve exactly?

On the one hand, a great deal of time and effort went on facilitating the online orders of customers. The organisation had listened to its customers well, and based on their wishes, and sometimes also demands, developed a webshop in which the customer process was pivotal.

Since 2017, more than 95% of the total turnover has gone through the Bidfood webshop. Online ordering has therefore become the standard, something unique in business-to-business (B2B) and within the food industry.

One of the reasons for this success is the online focus within the strategy that Bidfood has been following from the very start: an 'effortless & frictionless experience' of its customers online. In other words, serving its customers online as well as possible has been at the heart of its operations. This optimisation never stops, of course, and to this day continues to be one of Bidfood's cornerstones.

On the other hand, Bidfood also spends a huge amount of time and effort on helping its suppliers to become 'digitally minded'. From the start, Bidfood opened up its webshop for the 'online merchandise' of the products of its suppliers. A number of top brands already had some experience with online food commerce, through, for example, AH online. A majority of brands, however, were looking for opportunities. Through workshops and events, for example, and adapted online promotions, suppliers increasingly used Bidfood to give their products an online boost and to innovate jointly.

Phase 2: Setting up the Marketplace and Shop-in-Shop Strategy Rollout

After the success of this digital transformation, Bidfood continued with a further rollout of its platform strategy. Both customers and suppliers have different wishes and requirements regarding wholesale trade. Suppliers traditionally regard wholesalers as a carrier or logistics partner. Customers, on the other hand, expect much more from wholesalers, namely inspiration, advice, service and a shop experience as with a business-to-customer (B2C) webshop.

Bidfood thinks, therefore, that the business model of the traditional wholesale trade will eventually disappear, as the changing needs of both customers and suppliers are becoming increasingly complex.

Managing all these wishes and requirements within a single entity and on the basis of the wholesale model was becoming more and more complicated. Bidfood simply had to change with its customers and suppliers in order to be future proof.

In order to realise this, a marketplace model was launched alongside the traditional wholesale model.

Suppliers were given the possibility to open their own 'shop' within the Bidfood webshop, similar to the Rituals shop within the Dutch *de Bijenkorf* or the Nike shop within Zalando. The supplier is free to fill its shop with the relevant product range and content. In this way, the supplier also retains control at every level. The supplier provides its own shop-in-shop with products, marketing and merchandise and, if necessary, takes care of the delivery. Bidfood has been sharing certain data with its suppliers for years now. If they made use of the shop-in-shop concept, the data only increased further giving them more insight and clarity.

Suppliers were in this way able to use the Bidfood webshop, while still retaining control of the pricing, customer relations and fulfilment.

In practice, not every supplier was willing or able to have this. This is why Bidfood employs a growth model. Figure 1 shows where the

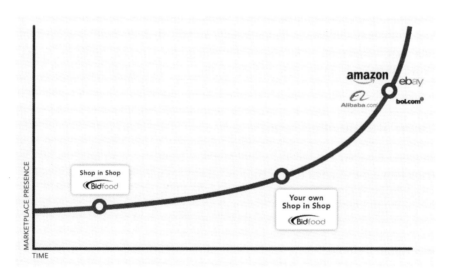

Figure 1.   Marketplace adoption.

shop-in-shops on Bidfood.nl are located on the adoption curve of top brand suppliers compared to the major marketplaces.

By the end of 2018, Bidfood had 30 shops live. These are grouped according to theme, seasons or, for example, the type of cuisine: the vegetarian shop, the BBQ shop and the vegan shop. Everything that customers may need for information or inspiration brought together in a single shop. The product is no longer central; what the customer wants is the starting point. Within this concept Bidfood looks for suppliers that can provide interesting products, advice and inspiration in relation to such a shop-in-shop. It also opened brand shops, but always from the viewpoint that they would have to provide added value for the customer.

Despite all these digital possibilities for suppliers, it turned out to be quite a challenge to keep them completely satisfied within the model of the traditional wholesaler. While suppliers developed an increasing need for their own route to market and for a direct contact with the customer, customers actually wanted to be part of a full-service inspirational food service company.

Suppliers want to have control over the margin and price, access to the customer and certainly access to the customer and transaction data. What's more, a marketplace is a separate business model that can have a serious impact on the traditional wholesale model.

In view of Bidfood's strong vision on platform development and the fact that a focus on customer needs remains a cornerstone of its operations, Bidfood has launched the third phase in its platform strategy.

Phase 3: Launching Foodl

Bidfood had already taken its first steps as a multisided platform, yet its suppliers continued to regard Bidfood chiefly as a logistics service provider specialised in processing transactions with a linear supply chain.

In order to truly realise a breakthrough in Food service, Bidfood decided to initiate a corporate start-up: Foodl.

While Bidfood continues to position itself as a full-service wholesaler for customers, Foodl is to be deployed alongside it as a separate business for the suppliers who wish to retain control themselves.

Why Foodl?

Bidfood was able to work on the digitalisation of its business early on. This is part of the reason that Bidfood has experienced such enormous growth in the hotel and catering market. A large part of its business, however, is still based more on traditional wholesale processes. Times are changing, and customers want to be in control even more, and not base their business on what the wholesale trade can offer. And everything as digital as possible. The supplier is constantly looking for innovation, and wants to learn and change on the basis of data and have a direct dialogue with the target group. And the target group, the progressive chef, expects nothing less. The chef always wants unlimited access to the latest products and knowledge in the most effortless of ways, in order to be able to constantly reinvent himself and his business. Foodl focuses completely on matching the needs and services between demand (the customer) and the supply (the food suppliers). Foodl wants to remove as much as possible all those barriers that a customer feels and experiences in the traditional wholesale sector. Convenience is central. By launching Foodl, Bidfood is again taking a step towards a future-proof business.

Foodl facilitates in the direct dialogue between supplier and chef. Foodl will keep a constant focus on innovation and convenience, looking at the total customer experience: service, advice, inspiration and, of course, the order. A good webshop cannot operate effectively without these four elements; however, within a platform they are even more essential in order

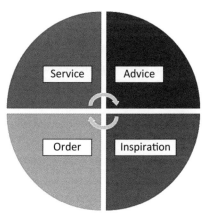

to give customers the right experience and providers the right tools.

In the past years, Bidfood has acquired the extensive experience necessary to develop a customer-driven organisation. Within Foodl, this knowledge is incorporated and combined with the knowledge and wishes of the providers.

An essential aspect of a food platform is that a customer can 'simply' place an order. The primary flow has to be right. In addition, there needs to be a perfect match between the inspiration the customer is seeking, the advice he or she wishes to receive and, of course, the necessary space for excellent service.

This book has referred to the customer loop, where a customer starts with a particular need, and if the experience is positive the transaction will then come about as a logical consequence.

Here are just a few of the questions that a hotel and catering customer may have:

Are there any upcoming events or holidays? Is this the start of the asparagus season? Now that I am starting up a new business. … How can I improve my profits? A chef is regularly faced with these sorts of questions for which he tries to find an answer. All these questions eventually lead to a transaction, providing that the part in-between is handled correctly. And that is precisely where Foodl comes in, as *the* online marketplace for entrepreneurs and chefs with a foodie mindset. On Foodl, finding and buying anything you might need is an extremely quick and easy process. The shopping experience ensures for ultimate ease and convenience with features for the 'smart chef' of today and the future.

The wishes and requirements of suppliers are changing considerably. As already indicated, they are looking for their own route to market. Foodl facilitates this. It gives them the possibility to learn to work within a platform environment. A provider can 'open' its own shop on Foodl, which helps it to learn about online merchandising, online sales and digital marketing within a webshop. Knowledge that is essential within a platform environment. The provider can carry out the deliveries itself or use the services of a third party, for example, PostNL or DHL.

Urban distribution is an important driver. The increase in online orders and the growing number of hotels and catering businesses have put considerable pressure on the logistics within city centres. If you consider the necessity for reducing CO_2 emissions, it is clear that change is necessary. There need to be future-proof solutions that focus particularly on urban distribution.

In summary, why Foodl?

- For the customer: easy-to-make choices, based on the customer's needs and the customer's demand for extreme online convenience.

- For the supplier: the supplier's own route to market, with direct contact and access to the customer via his own shop within a business ecosystem.
- For the changing urban distribution: innovative working practices and partnerships, taking into account the wishes of customers and providers.

Foodl goes one step further than just focusing on the product and facilitating the transaction. Foodl facilitates in matching a food supplier's services with a customer's needs. After all, the majority of the transactions start with a search, irrespective of the form it takes.

Foodl has been set up as a business ecosystem in which all e-commerce activities are connected with the logistics.

Foodl is an example of a B2B ecosystem: the knowledge of suppliers, the focus on the tremendous online convenience that you get from the larger webshops and the logistics combined within a single platform. The needs and wishes of the customer are central, not the product (Figure 2).

The facilitation of the learning curve is the most important in the first phase of Foodl. We will just have to wait and see when Foodl develops into a fully independent business.

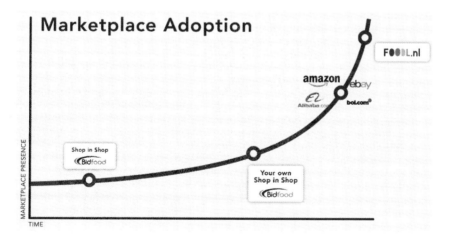

Figure 2.   Marketplace adoption in time

Phase 4: Complete Online and Logistical Integration

The next phase is already just around the corner. This will involve a complete integration of content, communication, inspiration and the transactions of individual businesses that are linked to one another. Customers look for total convenience, or, as described before, a frictionless and effortless experience.

The above will be necessary in order to achieve success. Many more partnerships will be established, with organisations working together and harnessing their forces. The step from order entry to new digital business ecosystems will be taken as a consequence. In other words, from doing digital to being digital.

Anouk Beeren
E-commerce & Marketing Director Bidfood Netherlands

Appendix 2

Dating Sites: An Example of a Multisided Platform*

The network applications form the basis for new start-ups and consequently for a new competitive proposition. These new start-ups will often have a single theme or product for a single sector, with which they wish to attract visitors (consumers) and link providers, often at website level. They then later expand the network contacts and facilities. The link is a match between supply and demand. But why is it based on products? A match can also be made based on personal needs or wishes, such as for a restaurant or meal (opentable.com), cinema or theatre performance, and also for a partner.

Dating sites, which aim to match the 'supply and demand', belong to the earlier applications in the third phase of the development of the network economy. On the basis of a wide range of elements, people can search and make contact with others. The strength of the matching model is based on there being plenty of demand and supply. The revenue model is based on the contributions of the 'members'. The services provided by these 'partner matching' sites have continued to improve. We now see the

---

*Information based on the article Modern Love, *The Economist*, 18 August 2018, p. 9 and 16 ff.

addition of videos, organised activities (a crossover between Internet dating and physical dating) and psychological questionnaires to help make better matches. The registration of the needs and wishes on the side of the 'demand' and registration of the available 'supply' has much improved. The addition of extra services such as psychological questionnaires, as well as get-togethers and holidays for singles has helped create a multisided platform. The various matching providers claim a success rate of more than 30%. The number of profiles distributed over these sites amounts to 10 million in the Netherlands. These figures may, of course, include double profiles. The Dutch market leader Relatieplanet contains approximately 5 million profiles.

Globally, Tinder is the most popular dating app, with already 50 million monthly users back in 2014. Tinder was founded in 2012 and is a worldwide platform, although the matches are made at a local level. Based on a profile and preferences, the platform determines the best fit, also on the basis of a person's current location. They can then make a contact request, which may or may not be accepted. Tinder is a smartphone-based app and allows users to swipe through a range of possible partners according to their location. After selecting the preferred partner, the person then has to wait for hopefully a positive reply (location-based matching). In 2014, some 12 million matches per day were realised through more than 1 billion *swipes*. Tinder is an example of matching supply and demand through an independent party. This makes Tinder a multisided platform, the basis for the network economy. With a successful platform such as Tinder it is very difficult for other parties to acquire a position alongside the market leader. In the Netherlands, we see this with Relatieplanet, as well as in other non-dating markets such as Bol.com, Booking.com, Dilveroo and Airbnb. In other countries, particularly in the United States, Amazon has created bonds with so many suppliers that independent companies scarcely have a chance. Amazon has the visitor numbers, the contacts and the market strength. Suppliers profit from this position of power. Bol.com as a broad provider also has a similar powerful market position (identical to Amazon's strategy). We also see this with the earlier mentioned dating sites where there is a powerful market leader and a number of followers, who try to offer other services in order to be distinctive and acquire a market position.

Dating Sites Results

In America, the relationships that have come about as a result of a matching site appear to last longer and result in happier couples than relationships that have come about offline. What's more, since the introduction of these dating sites, there has been a reduction in the divorce rate. The diversity and the specific wishes and needs for relationships are better realised (specific elements such as religion, background, impairment). It has also been suggested that online dating has an effect on society, on account of the far greater choice and subsequent unlimited number of partners. The market reach is greater, thereby reducing the relevance of factors such as nationality, skin colour and social class. The competition between the various dating sites concerns the number of registered users, as well as the algorithms (matching criteria and process) that aim to lead to a successful match. These new competitive relationships (and instruments) are also present in multisided platforms in other markets.

In China, Tantan is a popular website that attracts 20 million users and realises 10 million matches. However, due to cultural restrictions and limitations in the area of population diversity (many more boys than girls), the success rate is low. Tantan hopes to improve this by employing broader matching criteria within the algorithms so that everyone is able to receive a match.

Dating has always been a localised phenomenon, where people would choose from local partners. Now dating has become more of a concentrated activity, attracting people from far beyond one's own area. This leads to the disappearance of old boundaries and local communities. Dating has become a centralised process in the hands of a number of market leaders who determine the success (with their algorithms). The development of dating sites, with all their social consequences, the supply and the quality of the matching process, exemplifies multisided platforms and forms the basis for major disruptions.

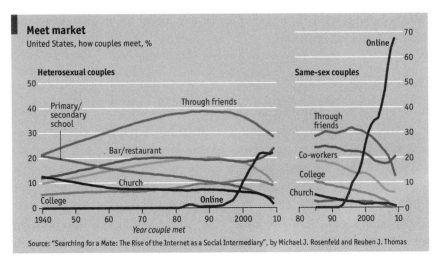

Figure 1.   Users of dating sites in the United States.

Source: The Economist, 18 August 2018, p. 17.

Tinder, the largest of the dating sites, has an estimated revenue of 4.6 billion (parent company Match Group). It is not surprising then that Facebook is going to provide a similar dating service. After all, Facebook is already a multisided platform with 3.5 billion active users worldwide (2018). Dating sites can be seen as an example of the traditional development in markets: a dominant party (independent) that matches supply and demand, where matches are determined by unseen algorithms.

The interpretation of Figure 1 for the Internet is relevant. Particularly articles that cannot be bought locally, of which the range is limited, are popular among online purchases. Discrete websites, such as for pornography, are also very popular due to the supposed privacy, comparable with the same-sex matches on the Internet.

Appendix 3

Differences between Various Forms of Collaboration

- **Webshops** are the usual way of selling products or services online. A company is the owner of the products that it sells to customers through its own website. Only two parties are involved: the seller and buyer.
- **Marketplaces** do not sell any products or services themselves; instead, they offer a platform on which sellers and buyers can carry out the transactions online. Examples of marketplaces are eBay, Uber, fiverr and Airbnb. So when you buy a product on eBay, you do not buy the product from eBay itself, but from a seller on eBay. From a legal standpoint, the sales agreement is between the seller and the buyer (not the market). It is the same concept as physical (offline) markets where you buy flowers and vegetables, for example.

  Marketplaces have various revenue streams. The most important is the commission (sellers or buyers pay a commission on a successful transaction). Other revenue streams include listing costs (sellers pay for offering their service/product), promotion costs (seller runs a promotion on the platform) and advertisements (banner or pop-up advertisements).

The marketplace concept is attractive for almost all industries. Requirements for a marketplace are that it offers standardised services/ products that do not need any physical examination prior to the purchase and do not involve major investments (prices below a few thousand dollars), portals for advertisements.

- **Multisided platforms** serve both sides of the market independently from one another: the consumer and the provider. The platform often takes the risk while facilitating the transaction. The connection between both market parties is established by the matching module that is based on a needs filter (consumer) and a supply filter (provider). The matching leads to products and services that can be delivered by the provider. The consumer chooses from the selected range of products or services. A 'normal' platform serves only one side of the market, usually the seller's, and only establishes a connection.

- **Portals** for advertisements are the modern version of the advertisement section of newspapers, and are very popular for property and second-hand products, as well as for customer-to-customer (C2C). The main difference with marketplaces is that the transaction takes place offline. The sellers list their products/services on the portal and potential buyers contact the seller. They carry out the transaction offline, for example, after examining the product. Examples of portals for advertisements include Craigslist, *eBay Kleinanzeigen* and *Immobilienscout* from Germany and *Marktplaats.nl* from the Netherlands.

  Portals with advertisements create value for the sellers by generating leads — buyers find sellers and then get in contact with them. The business model of portals is based on price lists (sellers pay to have their products included on the list), promotion costs (sellers pay to have their listings more prominently on the portal) and charging for leads (for example sellers pay €1 per lead — when a user clicks on the email or telephone button, this is counted as a lead).

- **Affinity marketing** is a form of reversed portal. On a company's own website they refer (via a link) to a seller that has realised the sale. With affinity marketing a fee is paid to the party who provided the lead.

- In order to make it easier to compare prices across webshops and marketplaces, a new e-commerce form was created, the so-called aggregators. These portals search through the Internet and collect information on the same product from various webshops (for example, the price of a new iPhone on Amazon, Coolblue and Bol.com). These portals help users to find the best price for various providers and generate a link to the supply directly from their website. By clicking on the provided link, the user will be referred to the webshop where the transaction can take place. An example of an aggregator is Idealo.de.

• Aggregators generate revenue through 'affiliate' deals. They charge webshops either for every click (cost per click) or for every purchase from a user that came about through the aggregator (cost per conversion).[1]

---

[1] *Source:* Based on an overview from marketplaceguru.de/differences-marketplaces-classifieds.